D0450128

How to Win
in Washington

To our sons Peter and Dan
and their families

How to Win in Washington

Very Practical Advice about Lobbying, the Grassroots, and the Media

Ernest Wittenberg and
Elisabeth Wittenberg

Basil Blackwell

Copyright © Ernest Wittenberg and Elisabeth Wittenberg 1989

First published 1989
Reprinted 1990

Basil Blackwell, Inc.
3 Cambridge Center
Cambridge, MA 02142, USA

Basil Blackwell Ltd
108 Cowley Road, Oxford, OX4 1JF, UK

Library of Congress Cataloging in Publication Data
Wittenberg, Ernest
How to win in Washington.
Bibliography: p.
Includes index.
1. Lobbying—United States—Handbooks, manuals, etc.
I. Wittenberg, Elisabeth. II. Title.
JK1118.W58   1989   324.4'0973   89–6930
ISBN 1–55786–034–3

British Library Cataloguing in Publication Data
A CIP catalogue record for this book is available
from the British Library.

Typeset by Hope Services, Abingdon, Oxon
Printed in Great Britain by
Billing and Sons Ltd, Worcester

Contents

Acknowledgments

Dozens of people, inside and outside of government, helped us write this book. All of them were busy, but they all found time to talk, to share their most interesting cases, to critique the drafts, and to spur us on to finish the work. The members of Congress who showed us how lobbyists appear from the vantage point of Capitol Hill were Senators Bob Dole, Jake Garn, Mark Hatfield, Orrin Hatch, Ernest Hollings, Daniel Patrick Moynihan, and Bob Packwood; and Representatives John Dingell, Sam Gibbons, Robert Michel, Charles Rangel, Morris Udall, and Jim Wright. Thanks to them and to all their administrative and legislative assistants, and appointment secretaries.

Then there were the veterans of countless Washington lobbying battles. Thanks, Susan Alvarado, Tommy Boggs, David Cohen, Stuart Eizenstat, James Fitzpatrick, Verrick (Vick) French, David P. Houlihan, James R. Jones, Tom Korologos, James O'Hara, Charls Walker, Anne Wexler, and Burt Wides. Unfortunately, Mr O'Hara will not be able to read that we are in his debt; he died in March, 1989.

We couldn't have done without the help of executives of the trade and professional associations. Our particular thanks to James Jay Baker, Martin Corry, Thomas A. Dine, Bob Frederick, Lynn Greenwalt, Bill Hamilton, Ray Hoewing, Jeffrey Joseph, Milton Mitler, Fred Mutz, Gary Shapiro, and John Zapp.

We gratefully acknowledge the insights gained from Stuart Butler, Philip Trezise, and Ben Wattenberg, of the think tanks.

Among the grassroots and public relations experts who sat still for grilling, we express appreciation to John Adams, Jack Bonner, Jeff Conley, Roger Craver, Bruce Harrison, John Meek, Howard Phillips, Richard Viguerie, and George Worden.

Many thanks to Arvin C. Blome and Bernard Ross for their thoughtful critiques of the manuscript, and Jim Fitzpatrick for his last-minute expert review of the proofs as an old Washington hand who can sniff out an error at 20 paces. Any errors that remain are, however, entirely ours.

In midstream we even tested the adage about changing horses and found it poor advice. We merged our 24-year-old consulting business with the E. Bruce Harrison Company, which gained not only a male vice-chairman but also half of a team heavy with book. Bruce and Patricia Harrison bore this major flaw in their new colleague with grace and never-failing help and enthusiasm for getting the product finished and on the street.

Writing a book tests one's friends, co-workers, and family. We needed constant encouragement and push, and research help. We'll never be able to thank them enough, but we'll try: David Yount, President of the National Press Foundation, who needed only pom-poms to win the cheerleading contest, Joe Harned, Executive Vice-President of the Atlantic Council of the United States, and possibly Washington's most urbane citizen, and Tom Mathews, the eminent consultant's consultant, who took us cross-country skiing in Yellowstone Park and said: "Now you're rested enough to get it finished." Thanks, Christine Adams and Amy DeLouise, for meticulous research. Peter Wittenberg deserves special thanks for soothing our computer angst, via telephone from Los Angeles. He also deserves special thanks for being our son. So does Dan Wittenberg. Our sons and their wives, who are the mothers of our grandchildren, all understood that we were bringing forth another offspring. Close to the end of the laundry list, there's our agent, Bill Kramer; Basil Blackwell's very perceptive editorial director, Peter Dougherty, and copy-editor, Dan Flanagan, a veritable magician. Finally – because it threatened to wipe out the entire manuscript if we didn't – thanks to our amazing Macintosh.

Prologue:
The Rustling of the Grassroots

The Bill of Rights gives you the *right* to lobby the government; it doesn't come with instructions. This book shows you how it's done. It provides a practical approach to influencing the decision-making process in Washington. The economic, political, and social decisions made in the capital of the United States affect billions of people, trillions of dollars, and the rules by which the world does business. Knowing how the place works, what motivates it, and how to have your voice heard in the proceedings are essential skills at every level of society today in every corner of the United States and around the globe.

Remarkably, all successful approaches to Congress follow a similar pattern. Whatever your business in Washington – tax relief, an environmental problem, civil rights or social issues, foreign trade or foreign policy – cases from the recent past can provide you with valuable insights to winning your own case, even if the subject matter is entirely unrelated to yours. This book will bring you right up to date on modern grassroots and lobbying practices.

You're going to find ideas, procedures, and methods used by the most effective lobbies to sway congressional opinion. For example, every business group drawing a bead on Washington should study how Chrysler stretched its economic impact into all 50 states to win the backing of a reluctant House and Senate for its controversial loan guarantee. The grassroots lessons of this case study are universal. If you intend to halt threatening legislation, the perfect role model is the National Rifle Association in its fight against gun-control bills. Usable examples abound in this book – not in the sense of precedents a lawyer cites to win a case, but as milestones of advocacy before Congress. In other words, these programs are proven winners. They worked!

Lobbying is a First Amendment right with a long history and techniques that are adaptable to the times. In this era of instant communications, the names, addresses, and specific interests of millions of people are available at the touch of a computer key. Touching another key will rally these millions to express their views to Washington. It's a grand parade for democracy – and it's growing bigger all the time, because of the way elected officials have to respond to the opinion of their constituents. The chances of *your* being involved are very high, whether as an extra, a bit player, or a star, and it is to your advantage to know the full route the parade will take before you start. It's a very well-marked trail, because under all the emotional, political and economic overlay, 90 percent of modern lobbying campaigns use the same methods. But the pattern doesn't become apparent until you put together the case histories of some of the most important recent struggles for the heart, mind, and vote of the Congress. The foundation of your campaign's success in Washington is neatly chiseled on a slab in front of the National Archives that says "The past is prologue."

Lobbying – an American Tradition

Arguably, lobbying is an indigenous American skill. It started before the birth of the Republic and has flourished ever since. Its most distinguished practitioner during colonial days was Benjamin Franklin. In 1757, members of the Pennsylvania Assembly appointed the Commonwealth's most famous man as their "agent" in an attempt to convince Parliament not to pass the Stamp Act. The Quakers raised £1,100 for his salary and expenses in London, but Franklin would accept only £500, a fee precedent few lobbyists have followed.

The Founding Father of traditional American lobbying was Dr Manasseh Cutler, a Yale-educated lawyer, scientist, and clergyman, who pulled off one of the greatest land deals of all time. Cutler had been a well-known figure in the War of Independence. He was the Minutemen's chaplain at Lexington and then became a physician in order to help the wounded for the remainder of the war.

In 1787, a group of former army officers, who were restless in the East incorporated as the Ohio Company and hired Cutler to get them unexplored government land in the West at bargain prices. After eight days of intensive lobbying of the leaders of the Continental Congress in New York on behalf of his client, he succeeded beyond his wildest dreams. Not only did Congress agree to sell the company 1.5 million acres at a paltry nine cents an acre, it also put up another 3.5 million acres for speculation. Cutler walked away with a deal that encompassed the future states of Ohio, Indiana, Illinois, Michigan, and Wisconsin.

Cutler did not rest on his laurels. As soon as the deal was cut, he hurried down to Philadelphia, where the Constitutional Convention was hammering out the shape of a new federal government. There he displayed the primary skills of the best lobbyists of any period – ingenuity, determination, and an ability to gain access. The fact that the proceedings were being conducted behind locked doors and that the delegates were pledged to secrecy didn't stop him for a minute. He couldn't reach them during business hours, so he socialized with them at night. Determined to ensure that the new constitution did not abrogate deals made with the previous government, he dined with James Madison, George Mason, Alexander Hamilton, and others. He also gained an audience with Benjamin Franklin, who proved so loquacious that aides had to remind him that there was a lid on news about the debates taking place at the convention. In the end, Cutler's clients were more than satisfied, for the new Constitution did indeed protect existing contracts.

The Cutler way of lobbying was the Washington way for almost 200 years. The rules were simple: gain access to the key legislators, who were the chairmen of the great committees in the House and Senate; convince them of the worth of your cause and let them push it through.

As Manasseh Cutler set out in a sulky for the Ohio River settlement of Marietta, the first Congress of the United States convened and slapped 50 percent tariffs on 70 different commodities to encourage and protect local manufacture in an economy that was 96 percent agricultural. The textile lobby had arrived as the first US industrial special interest group – and it's still going strong more than 200 years later, winning consistently with a coalition of manufacturing, agriculture, and labor. The issue hasn't changed much over two centuries – just the geography. The First Congress legislated against European textiles, the 100th against Asian. But even this enduring institution changed its methods of lobbying when a reform Congress shook up Washington in the mid-1970s, creating the current climate on the Hill.

The Watergate Watershed

The reform of Congress, oddly, can be traced directly to a bungled burglary on the night of June 17, 1972. Five men who worked for President Richard M. Nixon's re-election committee were caught red-handed in the Democratic Party's national headquarters, in the Watergate complex on the shores of the Potomac. Over the next two years the whole sordid story of deception, trickery, and money-laundering unravelled before the public's fascinated stare. The result was not only the first resignation of a sitting president, but the election in 1974 of a group of young, liberal, progressive, and fighting-mad members of the House and Senate. The principal losers were the "old bulls" – the Southern conservative committee chairmen, who lost much of the autocratic power they had wielded on Capitol Hill for generations.

The reformers put the old bulls out to pasture by smashing the congressional seniority system. From day one, these upstarts of the 94th Congress showed no patience with the established gospel of congressional gerontocracy, which held that junior members should "get along by going along" until they accumulated enough seniority to be granted admission to the inner circle of leadership. By allying themselves with the frustrated freshman class of the previous Congress, the reformers formed a voting bloc strong enough to stand Congress on its ear.

Instead of just watching the game being played by a few people in the leadership – the traditional way for beginners to behave – the freshmen dealt themselves winning hands in the varsity game. Their pattern for change was a dusty reform agenda written back in 1970 by the Democratic Study Group, a coalition of liberal Democrats, against just such a new day. To begin with, the reformers voted away some of the awesome power over legislation held by the chairmen, forcing the latter to make room at the legislative table for the junior members. The tax-writing House Ways and Means Committee, for example, had literally been a one-man show starring Chairman Wilbur Mills (D, Ark.) and lacking even a single subcommittee. After reform, it sported six newly minted subcommittees that spread the responsibility around, giving every member a share in fashioning the nation's tax and trade laws. "You can't imagine how exciting it was for a junior member to come onto Ways and Means with zero seniority and have a voice in the proceedings," remembers Rep. Charles Rangel, a New York City Democrat who joined the committee in 1975 after one term in Congress.

Then the reformers blew away the back-room cigar smoke by opening the entire legislative process to public view (except, of course, for national security matters). They invited the citizenry to sit in on congressional hearings; legislative mark-up sessions, where laws are actually written line-by-line; and, frequently, House–Senate conferences, where the differences between versions of the law are blended. The effect of these "sunshine laws" was to make the voters active players in all the steps of congressional decision-making. Before the sunshine laws, not even the staffs of some committees were allowed in the room when committee votes were taken – without a written record.

The democratization didn't put the committee chairmen out of business; there was still plenty of power to wield. They selected the witnesses and orchestrated the testimony for hearings, presided over the committee meetings, hired most of the staff, and controlled the subcommittee budgets. But the days of tyrannical control by the chairmen were definitely over.

By the time they were finished with their overhaul, the reformers had done nothing less than revolutionize the way legislative business is approached in the United States. And in the course of doing so, they forced a radical change in the ancient practice of lobbying.

Lobbyists, used to the cozy simplicity of dealing just with committee chairmen to get laws passed or stopped, suddenly had to find ways to convince hundreds of previously ignored legislators, whose votes now mattered on every issue. Veteran business lobbyist Charls Walker, who recalls getting changes made in the tax code during the Eisenhower years just by convincing two people – Speaker of the House Sam Rayburn and Chairman Wilbur Mills – now lobbies all three dozen members of the Ways and Means Committee.

Walker and other traditional lobbyists discovered that pressure from a legislator's home district was the key to post-Watergate lobbying. Lobbyists now had to harness voter power, congressional district by congressional district, to win a majority in committee balloting. The courting of the grassroots became a priority for every lobby, from the great corporations to the public interest groups. The grassroots had evolved from a figure of speech into a political reality.

Companies found that they could widen their impact on the Hill by cultivating networks of customers, suppliers, and employees in as many congressional districts as possible. These local voices could be organized into a chorus that would be heard in the right places in Washington when the need arose. Localization was crafted into its ultimate form by the manufacturers of the B-1 bomber, who gave their political consultants equality with the purchasing agents in the selection of suppliers and parts manufacturers for the aircraft. Eureka! They gave a stake in the B-1's future to people in all 435 congressional districts, assuring continued production regardless of expert criticism by rivals and other opponents. Nonprofit organizations and professional societies, unions and farmers, city and state governments, public interest groups and foreign governments – all became skilled in vote counting, demographics, and the application of voter pressure on Congress.

In the new climate, millions of people whose civic awareness had stopped with seventh-grade civics found all kinds of reasons to get in touch with their own representatives in Washington when a bill was on the line. The entire country – an area Washington knows mostly as "Outside the Beltway" – now was watching Congress, ready to join the action.

This triangulation system – lobbyists selling ideas to the folks back home, so the folks back home will convince their elected officials that the lobbyists' ideas deserve support – was nice and simple at the beginning. A few letters, a couple of phone calls – *vox populi*. Then high technology came into the picture, and the Capitol post office and telephone system are still struggling with what IBM hath wrought. As the computer-generated voice of the people was heard throughout the land, the mail coming into congressional offices expressing positions for and against major legislation often had to be weighed instead of counted.

With the reform of Congress there was also a change in the type and numbers of people who took up lobbying. It became a much more open business, one that was even being taught in colleges. The new breed, younger men and women whose expertise is less in friendship and backroom politics than in substantive issues, are much more open about describing their occupation. The usual conversation-opener at the shrimp-bowl at an embassy reception is, "What do you do?" The answer used to be, "I'm a legislative liaison officer" or some other contortion to obfuscate the job description. Today they say directly, "I'm a lobbyist."

The resident population of lobbyists is augmented daily by plane- and train-loads of commuting business men and women, not to mention the thousands of concerned citizens who take their commitment to social issues seriously and want to exercise their right to influence the legislature in person.

While lobbying is still not exactly an equal-opportunity field, neither is it any longer an almost all-male preserve. That attractive young woman on the tennis court, three years out of college, could be a full-fledged lobbyist for a *Fortune* 500 company. In the 1950s, she would have been allowed to type the position papers.

The new-style lobbyists are very happy to be constrained by another post-Watergate reform. No longer do lobbyists have to sneak money to their favorite legislators – like the favor-seekers who stuffed hundred-dollar bills into the overcoat pockets of Senator Herman Talmadge of Georgia so he wouldn't have to touch the money (a fact that came out in some messy divorce proceedings). All money that changes hands in the political process has to be accounted for publicly.

If lobbying has become more widespread, so that any number can play, it has also become more competitive. Today, as never before, the lobbyist must be knowledgeable and prepared – for his or her opponents on the other side of an issue almost certainly will be both.

If you are starting a lobbying campaign, are active in a public interest group, are serving as liaison between city or state government and the federal presence, looking after the interests of a government or business, or simply representing a small, local group with a federal case – you can benefit from detailed advice on the practicalities of winning legislative battles. How do you organize a lobbying campaign that will have a chance of being successful? What factors make the difference? How do you gain access to the decision-makers? How do you locate allies? How in the world *do* you get the voters back home riled up and mobilized for action? Where do you find a lever long enough to move Congress? How do you groom a witness to be effective at a congressional hearing? What role do the news media play in the process, and how do you communicate with them? How can you motivate members of a lobbying coalition to do something more than lend their names to a letterhead?

Since the mid-1970s, a good many insightful people have faced and answered these questions successfully. To harvest the fruits of their experiences, we buttonholed scores of friends, presumed on acquaintances, and depended on the kindness of strangers. In almost all cases, our queries elicited enthusiastic and candid responses – a fact that may shock that segment of the public which still considers lobbying a black art, not to be discussed in polite society.

From these responses and from interviews with congressional leaders – as well as from lessons learned in our 26 years of working in Washington as consultants, public relations counselors, and lobbyists – we have distilled a set of strategies and tactics indispensable to anyone who enters the maze of contemporary lobbying and grassroots mobilization, even at the edges. We can't guarantee that you will win in Washington if you follow the guidelines laid out in the following chapters. We can guarantee, however, that if you ignore them, your lobbying campaign will have an unnecessarily rocky road to follow.

Good luck!

Part I
Opening Moves

1

Setting the Pattern for Success

The Winning Pattern

There is a distinct pattern to winning in Washington. It starts the moment you arrive at National or Dulles with a briefcase, polished shoes, and a vision of making a dent in the legislative process. The briefcase may contain documentation for a brilliant new law, or all the reasons why someone else's harebrained schemes must be stopped cold.

On any given early-morning flight, perhaps half of the passengers are on their way to deal with some problem with the Federal government. You're way ahead, however, just by knowing that there is a pattern to follow to come out on top. You can play variations on the theme – maybe even take a shortcut here or there – but you would be ill-advised to stray very far from the blueprint.

Keep in mind that business people, labor union officials, farmers, public interest advocates – even the people who market the legislative package for the President of the United States – all approach Capitol Hill in exactly the same way. They may see different people, present different views, and illuminate issues from a different angle, but if their approach is going to have a chance it must follow the same basic formula that you will be using. Alone, or with an army of consultants, every winning lobbyist must do the following.

Define the issue Naturally, your issue is of overriding importance. But in order to get on the agenda in Washington you must make it understandable. The goals should be clearly stated and logically presented in no more than two double-spaced pages – a draft the size of a novel frightens people off. And if it takes you more than three minutes to explain your basic concept to a senator's legislative assistant, you need to do more editing. Ideally you should be able to state the gist of your concept in headline length, and then sufficiently relate its effects on the environment, the public weal, or the reelection chances of the senator whose office you're visiting. Holding the attention of a busy Hill audience is no easy task.

According to former Oklahoma congressman James R. Jones, who once headed the House Budget Committee, where there are no easy solutions or quick answers, any explanation that takes longer than *two* minutes is a weak defense or a wasted offense. You'll have more time than that to explain the concept, but the opening is crucial. The assistant may still be listening to you after the buzzers go off and the lights flash to call the Senate into session, but her mind will also be on the big floor-speech her senator is going to make in the next hour.

Compressing complex ideas into a form that fits somewhere between the baseball scores and the weather report is a daunting task, but in Washington, the shorter the initial presentation, the better. The full explanation, the position papers, the graphs, the scientific backup, the public opinion polls available to support your headline will be used – but only if you first get the attention of the legislator.

Research the issue Your goal should be to gather more facts than you'll ever need to present a reasonable case. Count on opposition developing, because in Washington it always does. The issue most likely to win is one that is very narrowly defined, of utmost interest to one voter and one legislator, and attachable as an amendment to any bill that happens to go by. One other qualification: it's best if the issue is of absolutely no interest to anyone else. If it is, you've developed your first opponent or your first ally.

Even if you can't identify who your enemies will be, show great respect for the thoroughness of these phantoms in preparing a case against your ideas. Expect all enemies to be smart enough to know at least as much as you do about the case you are making, and to be able to punch holes in your arguments. They'll need only one opening, one false note in your theory, to grill your program like shish kebab.

Remember that these very bright people – don't imagine even for a moment that they aren't – will be working to convince the same people you'll be talking to that the Republic can survive admirably without your legislation.

Recruit allies Find as many supporters as possible, and then find some more. You're looking for anyone with even a remote interest in seeing your side win. That goes for individual voters back home, trade and professional associations, experts on your side of the issue, and public figures from film stars to athletes and astronauts. Congress is a representative body, and its members are far more likely to take positions they know to be important to a good proportion of the people they represent. The first question you'll be asked is, "What kind of support have you got?" To push your program through Congress, your sponsor will need to wind up with 217 other members of the House, plus 51 senators, whose constituents think you have a good idea. That's not exactly a piece of cake on any issue. Keep looking for allies until you find them in every state and congressional district. In practice, you'll have a nucleus of allies on board before you approach a potential congressional sponsor – but with allies, as with money, you never have enough.

Find a congressional sponsor Nothing important happens on the Hill until a member of Congress becomes interested and decides to make a serious commitment to a project. Matching the right member with the right issue is essential, but that's the easy part. Getting the member to take up your cause is harder – but remember, it's being done every day. And by the way, before you start knocking at congressional doors other than those of your own elected officials, be sure to register as a lobbyist. Although the Lobbying Act of 1946 is famous around Washington for its vagueness and lack of enforcement, don't be lulled into noncompliance by its toothlessness. Make it a matter of pride to tell the Congress (and the rest of the world through the publicity it gets) the nature and financial details of your legislative interest. Registration identifies you better than a calling card, and you'll avoid possible embarrassment.

Raise the visibility of the issue The ears of senators and representatives are sensitively attuned to the rustle of the grassroots. Their support for an issue depends largely upon what their constituents have to say about the proposal. And because the voters get their information through newspapers and TV and radio coverage, you'll have to find a way to interest the media out where the grassroots grow. If they're talking about your issue back home, you can be sure it will be heard in the congressional office buildings in Washington before very long. Just in case the staff or the member didn't happen to read the hometown papers the day your issue was featured, thoughtfully send along a copy of the clipping.

Support the issue in public hearings The committee and subcommittee members who will decide the fate of the project will only be convinced of its need and practicality by direct questioning of your witnesses, who must know what to expect and how to answer. Few spectacles are more embarrassing than that of an unprepared witness being shrunk to microscopic size before your very eyes by a probing member of Congress. Make sure that everyone who testifies on your side is precise, knowledgeable, courteous, and unflappable.

Monitor the issue tenaciously right through the legislative process When your enthusiasm flags, the issue is in trouble. No one else will be as interested in your case as you are. If you promise your congressional sponsor strong help from the grassroots and don't deliver, don't bother coming back next time. Follow-through work needs constant vigilance, support, and bolstering all the way through the House and Senate to the President's desk.

Washington is a vast stage on which thousands of actors compete for the attention of just three audiences: Congress, the executive branch, and the media. Not every issue is larger-than-life. It may concern millions of people or billions of dollars, or special citizenship for a tennis-player before the next Davis Cup matches. The public business knows no bounds. On Capitol Hill the world and everything in it are neatly assigned to no more than 15 standing committees in the Senate and 22 in the House, whose chairmen decide which issues are important enough to be discussed. The committees on both sides of the Capitol – and when you speak to a House member you refer to the Senate as the "upper house" entirely at your own risk – do the same work and cover everything under the sun, although the names don't always match. (The late Theodore Green, as a 90-year-old senator from Rhode Island, said he could only remember that his committee was called Foreign Relations and not Foreign Affairs, like the House committee, because senators had relations but were too old to have affairs.)

On a reasonably quiet Tuesday in June 1988 – "quiet" because there was no major national or international crisis and no significant votes were scheduled in the House or Senate – there were 38 announced public hearings in the two chambers. Among the diverse subjects dealt with at these hearings were nutrition programs, antitrust regulation, drug-abuse problems in the military, appropriations for foreign operations, AIDS research, sports fishing and hunting, hazardous waste reduction, health care needs for the elderly, and transportation of natural gas. And countless other issues were waiting in the wings. No issue will be heard until its visibility is high enough to convince the schedulers that it is of burning concern to the electorate.

A billion-dollar industry in Washington concerns itself with trying to do exactly that. Lobbying firms, public relations companies, lawyers, trade association executives, company representatives, and public interest groups are all trying to win a precious time-slot for their issues on the appointment schedule of one legislator, or, through a hearing, of an entire committee. You must either compete with them or work with them. In any case, you must always remember that your voice is only one of many, and it's up to you to make it heard.

The Ten Commandments of Lobbying

All of the advice contained in the following chapters can be distilled into the Ten Commandments of Lobbying. Display them over your desk, on the photocopy machine, and near the water cooler. The lobbyist who violates them risks the loss of his goal.

I Thou shalt speak only the truth, and speak it clearly and succinctly; on two pages and in 15-second sound bites.

II Thou shalt translate the rustle of thy grassroots into letters, phone calls, and personal visits.

III Thou shalt not underestimate thy opponent, for he surely packeth a rabbit punch.

IV Help thy friends win reelection; but in victory, dwelleth not on the power of thy PAC.

V Thou shalt know thy issue and believe in it, but be ready to compromise; half a loaf will feed some of thy people.

VI Runneth not out of patience. If thou can not harvest this year, the next session may be bountiful.

VII Love thy neighbor; thou wilst need him for a coalition.

VIII Study arithmetic, that thou may count noses. If thou can count 51, rejoice. Thou shalt win in the Senate.

IX Honor the hard-working staff, for they prepare the position papers for the members.

X Be humble in victory, for thy bill may yet be vetoed.

2

Gaining Entry – and Access

Getting a Foot in the Door

Congress is open, accessible, and tangible. You can talk to any member's staff, and from the courtesy and interest they show you, you will go away believing that you have the persuasive gifts of a Daniel Webster. You can also participate in the shaping of legislation up to the final outcome, because almost every step in the process is carried out in public view.

As a lobbyist stalking Congress, you will wear out a great deal of shoe leather on the beat, because there is no central place to make your case unless you are the President of the United States delivering a State of the Union address. You'll have to make friends (or foes) one at a time.

But even if you're on your way to Washington because some regulation is sheer dribble and your blood pressure has jumped 15 points trying to prove it to an independent agency, Congress is still the right address. Independent agencies are independent of everything except Congress, which created them, oversees how they handle public policy, and, most importantly, sets their budgets. Some legislator will happily take up your cause and fire a few salvos to get the attention of the regulators. The Hill is, hands down, the best pen-pal of the agencies and executive departments. In 1986 the Navy alone responded to 27,700 written queries and answered 125,000 phone calls from Congress – most of them inspired by constituents with problems.

While the deliberations in Congress are open to anyone who can pass the X-ray machines at the entrances, the decision-making process at the other end of Pennsylvania Avenue is closed, inaccessible, and invisible to the public – regardless of which administration is in power. When a presidential decision is made, only two or three people around the chief executive know the reasons that prompted the action. Even most of the input on which the decision is based is shielded from the public view, coming as it does from many people in many government agencies along the way. Executive decisions are greatly influenced by career bureaucrats, most of whom are almost impossible to lobby in person.

So focus your efforts and resources on Congress. If what you are doing is important enough, and if you faithfully follow the winning pattern, they'll soon hear about your ideas at 1600 Pennsylvania Avenue. The tenants of the White House don't live in a vacuum.

Even the White House must constantly lobby Congress. The President of the United States always needs grassroots help to turn ideas into legislative action. Some presidents, such as Jimmy Carter, never did get the hang of it; others, such as Lyndon Johnson and Ronald Reagan, were completely at home with it. Johnson, an accomplished arm-twister and lapel-grabber, ran Medicare through the House and Senate in less than a year, over the virulent objections of the American Medical Association, principally by cornering senators and representatives and convincing them one by one that he had an issue that was popular with the electorate.

Ronald Reagan similarly used grassroots support in lobbying a reluctant Congress to lower taxes in 1981 in the face of a huge government deficit. Of course, lower taxes are an irresistible issue. Voters clamor for it. On the other hand, the choice of a Secretary of Defense does not arouse the average voter. So the Bush Administration in early 1989 couldn't muster enough grassroots enthusiasm to support the President's nomination of John Tower over the objections of a balking Senate.

While the President has many more advantages than you will ever have, the basics of getting a program through the Hill are exactly the same for everyone. You'll need a coalition of allies to lobby along with you in an effort to show Congress that someone is in favor of your issue in that huge Washington exurb called America. It also helps enormously if your subject is of interest to the news media. Newsworthiness raises an issue's priority on the public agenda and helps to win congressional attention. The average citizen becomes aware that an issue is important or pressing when it makes the morning paper or the evening news. In this regard, Washington officials are no different from anyone else.

Finding friends on the Hill

Approaching Congress is a little like starting on a crossword puzzle. You go down the line until you find a word that you know, and work your way up, down, and across from there. The "words" you know in the congressional puzzle are your own representative and your state's two senators. If the case concerns their electoral area, either directly or tangentially, the doors of their offices will always be open, and even your Labrador retriever won't show as much intelligent interest in what you have to say. The member's staff will take pains to provide the kind of Washington advice to make your program achievable. And if your own representative or senator isn't on the right committee, he or she will refer you to the office of a friendly colleague who is.

The reason for all this attention is, of course, that you are a voter, and you may even represent whole groups of voters. The service potential of a member of Congress on behalf of a constituent knows few bounds. In most offices, constituent service comes first, legislation second — because no matter how eminent a legislator becomes, how much she is courted by the President of the United States and her words of wisdom and foreign policy voting record are treasured by the Prime Minister of Great Britain and the corporate giants of the world, she couldn't have done it without the voters. And she knows it. If you are an employer in the district, so much the better; your legislative interest is probably going to help bring or keep jobs.

Staying right on top of the news from home is of first priority throughout Congress, from the leadership to the bottom of the ladder. Illinois representative Robert H. Michel, the Republican leader of the House, is never too busy with high politics and nose-counting and White House strategies to ignore the important headlines from Peoria — and in particular, those dealing with its largest employer, Caterpillar Tractor. He stays close to his roots. So did the late Henry "Scoop" Jackson, a senator from Washington

State. Known worldwide as an expert on foreign affairs and defense, Jackson was scathingly labeled the Senator from Boeing by his opponents because of his unflagging activity on behalf of the Seattle-based aerospace manufacturer.

Starting with the home team is a great idea, but there is one caveat. If you know in advance that the people who represent you are fully committed against the cause you advocate, forget it. You wouldn't go to North Carolina senator Jesse Helms, a born and born-again believer in tobacco crops, for advice on getting smoking prohibited, for example. There are better ways to spend your time – such as determining how to get access to members who are philosophically more attuned to your point of view.

The constituent advantage

Congressmen forget where they came from at their own peril. The classic example used by people on the Hill to frighten themselves into frequent trips home is that of ex-senator J. William Fulbright. As chairman of the Foreign Relations Committee, Fulbright was a household name in every part of the world – but when he became better known in Arkansas for his international scholarship funds and expertise in foreign policy than for his interest in the economy of Little Rock, the voters ended his Senate career. And when Al Ullman, who rose to the chairmanship of the mighty Ways and Means Committee, became too absorbed in his committee assignments to pay frequent visits to the voters in Oregon, his absence became the campaign issue that defeated him.

Every congressman knows that constituent service is the mainstay of the office. There are many ways to be helpful when a voter is trying to get something done in the complex federal establishment. What's urgent to the voter is important to the congressional office. Equipped with three offices operating in his Manhattan district, Representative Charles Rangel (D, NY) deals with 1,500 requests per week, ranging from funding for a day-care center to getting an appointment to Annapolis for a young woman. The office of Representative Stan Parris (R), whose Virginia district borders Washington, specializes in the problems of federal employees, and constituent outrage at the TV blackout of Washington Redskins' home games spurred Parris to lead a successful congressional campaign to lift the veil over the games. With four offices scattered around the huge expanse of New Mexico, Senator Pete Domenici (R) does a land-office business in the Mexican-border city of Las Cruces, where the residents turn to him for help with immigration, Social Security, and Medicare problems.

When Picker International, of Cleveland, was on the verge of losing a $21 million Veterans' Administration hospital contract for CAT scanners, the company was steered to the offices of Representative Edward F. Feighan (D) of Cleveland and Ohio's two Democratic senators, Howard Metzenbaum and John Glenn. Galvanized by the potential loss of 300 jobs in employment-hungry Ohio because of a technical misunderstanding in the bidding process, this mini-coalition reopened communications between the VA and Picker. In less than three weeks, the contract went to Cleveland – saving the jobs and, potentially, at least 300 votes each for the elected officials who had stepped in to save the day.

While Picker came to Washington for redress, it's not essential to make the trip to start things going. Effective contact can be made right at home. Every member of Congress maintains at least one office back in the district, staffed with able personnel who are steeped in local as well as national issues and are just waiting for you to drop in or call. And they will act fast, in full coordination with their colleagues on the Hill. Then, too, the legislator often returns to the district and probably will have more time for you there than in Washington.

When you do go to Washington, don't believe the old saw that the capital is a Tuesday-through-Thursday town. Mondays and Fridays are not good days to plan fancy congressional receptions, because many of the members are back home meeting with constituents, but they are great days for you to do business on the Hill. The staff is in full working order and has the time to see you – maybe even to have lunch.

Also remember that long days are the rule in Washington. Even if you're not a VIP, your phone calls will get returned – although perhaps not until after 7.00 PM. If you're gone by that time, you'll be out of luck. The next time you see the person you were trying to reach, you'll be told that the return call was made, but you obviously left your office early that day.

Convincing the staff

Never underestimate the member's staff or the help they can give you. From the appointment secretary who can find a "window" in her boss's fully booked calendar to the legislative assistant who can guide you through the complexities of designing a bill and getting it into the hopper and the administrative assistant who can make the introductions to the people you have to see in order to win, the staff is crucial to your success. No less an authority than Bob Dole, the Republican leader of the Senate, holds that it is *better* to see the staff first. "If you get the staff interested, you're on your way," he points out. "They analyze the issue, they brief the member, and when you see your representative or senator after that, he or she already knows your objectives and can decide on the spot how best to help you. Most of the time you waste a whole step by insisting on seeing the member personally at that first meeting."

In many ways the staff will be an even tougher audience than the member, because they will be assigned to thoroughly review the material your case is based upon. The member of Congress most certainly is going to ask his staff to make an evaluation and advise him of the merits and demerits.

As the first people to judge the viability of your ideas, the staffers represent your first big hurdle. They will be polite but realistic. If they recommend something that turns out to be factually flawed, their reputations will go down the tube. You must give them the pros *and* the cons of the issue. Who stands against you on this matter? Who will benefit; who will lose? What is at stake for the other side? Stuart Eizenstat, once Jimmy Carter's chief domestic advisor and now a lawyer in Washington, doesn't even start one-on-one discussions of his client's case with anyone who can have an impact upon it until he knows the opposition's case perfectly. "I prepare for it the way I get ready to face a jury in a court of law. The members of Congress will be the jury, and unless I know exactly on what the other side is basing its case upon, I can't defend."

Before you visit a congressional office, draw up an account, using a credit-and-debit ledger, a legal pad, or a computer. Write down what you have going for you and what you have going against you. Be brutally honest with yourself. Are the facts as they stand now in your favor? If not, can your enthusiasm, your diplomacy, your persistence, outweigh the facts? Are you going with the spirit of the times, or are you working against it? David Cohen, one of the architects of the anti-Vietnam War lobbying, has said about working with Congress. "You are very often promoting an issue that is against the prevailing *zeitgeist*. But it's possible to change the mood of the country if you work at it."

Access: Friendship, Contributions, and PACs

In the language of Washington, *access* and *entry* are not interchangeable. *Entry* takes you into the building and carries you as far as the outer offices of the representatives and senators. *Access* takes you the rest of the way – to the appointment to sit down with the official and discuss starting a bill, stopping a bill, or getting support for your legislative ideas.

Access is the currency of lobbyists in Washington, and there are various ways to earn it. The surest is to be a constituent. Another is to be the representative of a vast number of voters, such as the membership of the American Association of Retired Persons (AARP). Still another is personal friendship. If you've gone to school with the member, if you're on the same board of directors for a charity, if you're her doubles partner or if you were the sponsor of his membership in your country club, your calls will be answered and it will turn out that someone has unexpectedly canceled an appointment that you are welcome to fill.

If you haven't got any of these advantages, your name should be known in the office as a contributor to the official's reelection fund. It's a matter of recognizing that the official is in the Capitol at the pleasure of the constituents and must reapply for the job every two or six years. It is an expensive, seemingly endless, and somehow demeaning process. As the wife of a former Virginia representative confided to us at a local, badly attended fund raiser at which guests left money in small checks at a table at the entrance, like the donations at an old-fashioned Irish wake, "Sometimes I dream that I have a husband who doesn't look for a job every two years."

Contributions

Private campaign financing has always been part of the American political scene, even if no history book mentions the dear friends of the candidates who paid for the broadsides that proclaimed "Tippecanoe and Tyler Too", or for the obligatory torchlight parades required wherever a nineteenth-century candidate gave a speech. And surely it wasn't the League of Women Voters who staged the Lincoln–Douglas debates.

All these unremembered people understood two things that were as true then as they are now: first, it's expensive to run for office; and second, as lobbyist Tom Korologos has said, democracy is not a spectator sport. If you want to have a hand in shaping the nation, you must get into it with more than your one vote on the Tuesday after the first Monday in November.

The leading lobbyists make no bones about the fact that they personally contribute everything the law allows and then sponsor fund-raisers to find other contributors. The Washington consensus is that money – used in legal ways – is an absolutely essential ingredient for operating successfully on the Hill. The operative word, again, is *access*.

A well-stocked reelection fund is like a security blanket to an incumbent. If a senator has, say, $2 million in the bank two years before the next election, the mere existence of all that money in a campaign fund will frighten away many potential challengers of stature. So fund-raising is a year-round activity, and those who knock at the door to make an impact on the legislative system do well to take this fact into consideration.

What the laws allows from individual donors is a maximum of $1,000 per congressional candidate in a primary and again in a general election, with a $25,000 limit on any person's total contributions in a year. The rule of thumb on campaign contributions is: Give, but don't expect to get a quid pro quo. Be content that you are probably on a list of friends whose opinions will be listened to on a priority basis. Your support isn't going to change a legislator's vote when the two of you disagree, but you'll very likely get an opportunity to tell the member or a key staffer that you think they are dead wrong, and why. If the member is undecided on the issue that interests you, and there is no particular grassroots pressure on it from the district – who knows? Your eloquence may win a vote for your side.

PACs

The generosity of Political Action Committees (PACs) is limited by law to $5,000 per candidate in the primary and that much again in November. The number of candidates that a PAC may help in one year is limited only by the number it wants to help and the current state of its treasury.

PACs were created in response to the funding excesses exposed in the Watergate scandals. As they proliferated, however, PACs became the target of widespread criticism. Common Cause, the public interest watchdog that stopped the delivery of those comforting corporate million-dollar Care packages in the first place by lobbying successfully for a new law, now says, sarcastically, about the PAC system, "We have the best Congress money can buy."

Charls Walker, who with Edmund Muskie cochaired a study of PACs for the Twentieth-Century Fund, likes PACs.

"The more I studied the financing of congressional campaigns, I concluded that by accident in 1974 we had stumbled onto as good a system as you can get," he explains. "What do you want in a congressional campaign? You want it open and above board. You don't want brown bags filled with money, and you don't want a senator to be owned by so and so.

"We had that sort of thing in the past. Because of the way the laws were, some fat cat with a hell of a lot of money could buy a lot of influence. The PACs, by limiting contributions to $5,000 – or $10,000 when you include the primary – have put members in a position where they don't have to depend on any one person, a few people or the people in any one company."

Though campaigns are more expensive than ever before and more private money is going into them, contributions now are strictly regulated and reported. Corporations, labor unions, and trade and professional groups cannot make direct contributions. Their employees or members make voluntary contributions through the PACs.

PACs represent a significant force in American election campaigns. Of all 535 senators and representatives, less than 5 percent turn away

PAC contributions. These holders of very safe seats feel that even with the limitations on their contributions, PAC members may feel that they have purchased an advantage over other, less affluent, citizens.

Some industry groups have found it advantageous to arrange delivery of PAC dollars from their member companies in tandem. This makes it obvious that a particular industry has come up with a hefty sum for a favorite candidate – most likely an incumbent. One well-financed member of Congress remarked that his vote is not for sale even though he accepts contributions. "The people who help in my campaign do so because they like my stand on the issues."

He is quite correct: a vote is seldom bought. No PAC would put its money into the war chest of a legislator who is dead set against its ideas of government. James G. O'Hara, who has been on both sides, as a representative from Michigan and a lobbyist, thinks that the influence of campaign contributions is overemphasized: "By the time someone is elected to Congress, they have pretty well established their philosophy of government. They have run and won on that philosophy as conservatives, liberals, Democrats, Republicans. The money comes in because of their records. You give to the guy who believes as you do.

"It is a crazy idea to think that legislators vote whichever way the money comes in. Congress may have 500 to 600 votes in a session. Damn few of them have much to do with philosophy of government. A lot of them are issues between contending commercial interests. But if one of the contenders is a contributor and one is not, and the vote is considered a toss-up or throw-away issue, members are apt to go along with the name they recognize from the form that was sent to the Federal Elections Commission."

Very few people think the current system is perfect, but attempts to get congressional elections funded like presidential elections, via public subscription on income-tax forms, have never won much support. Retired senator Robert Stafford, one of the sponsors of legislation that would have created a campaign checkoff on individual tax forms, says that although the public has the general impression that PACs are an evil influence, "a single $5,000 contribution doesn't mean all that much. I would guess that the senator often doesn't even know who gave him that money."

PACs are formed by people with interests in common. Doctors

have them and lawyers and bankers have them. The AFL-CIO has them – as a matter of fact, it had the original PAC, the Committee on Political Education (COPE), which provided the model for the rest of the country. Business caught up fast after the election laws changed: the Business-Industry Political Action Committee (BIPAC) is the private-enterprise version of COPE, and 80 percent of the money it raises goes into political education of members of individual company PACs.

Most of the 4,268 PACs that took part in the 1988 election cycle were associated with corporations and labor unions. However, all kinds of specialized causes also shell out dollars through PACs in the hope of pushing ideas into the mainstream. Committees such as the Alice B. Toklas Lesbian/Gay Democratic Club and the Concerned Romanians for a Strong America put their money on the noses of sympathetic candidates. A group of Texas high-school football coaches made grassroots history in 1985 by starting a political action committee aimed at letting them call signals in the state legislature. They were mad at the governor, who had instituted a "no pass, no play" rule that benched some of their top players.

The explosive growth of PACs has triggered a national debate. To some, PACs represent the flowering of democracy – a way to encourage more and more people to back the political system and their own ideas with dollars. Others are convinced that PACs mean the domination of Congress by the special interests. Senator David Boren, the Oklahoma Democrat who is championing another change in campaign financing, objects to, among other aspects, the narrow focus that PACs force upon the candidates: "A PAC does not judge a senator or congressman on his or her overall record or personal integrity. It does not balance the entire record to see if it serves the national interest. It rates the member solely on how he voted on bills affecting the particular financial interest group or single-issue constituency."

The jury is still out, so stay tuned. But in the meantime join a PAC, start one, or make contributions on your own. Contributing is quicker – and in the longer run, cheaper – than getting elected to the board of a charity as a way of meeting a member of Congress.

Honoraria

While it lasts, there is a third way – besides individual contributions and PACs – to use money on the Hill. Congress permits its members to earn up to $2,000 per engagement as honoraria for speaking dates to private groups. The House limits this type of income to 30 percent of the member's annual salary; the Senate to 40 percent. It might be a keynote speech at a trade association convention in California, a luncheon speech at a meeting of a company board of directors in midtown Manhattan, or (as we have frequently arranged) a seminar lecture a few blocks from the Capitol. The rule is that these are not lobbying occasions, but speaking for money is a controversial program and is likely to disappear if and when Congress votes itself a pay raise.

Making a contribution memorable

How do you make contributions gracefully? Like bodily functions and religion, money is never discussed directly with the member. In each office, one or two staffers are designated to manage the reelection fund – and even with them, money is not mentioned in so many words. In any case, it is illegal to hand over cash on federal property.

The operative phrase is, "I'd like to do something to help in the next election." In the next mail you will receive an invitation to a fund-raiser, anything from a $25 Western-style bull roast to a $1,000 full-scale black-tie dinner honoring a senator. If you forget to put the check in the mail, you'll find a place to put the envelope when you show up at the event.

The larger PACs, in making contributions at or near the legal maximum, seldom let the mailman deliver the good news. The presentation frequently becomes a ceremonial occasion back home that connects the contribution with the grassroots. The big national PACs, with millions of dollars to spend and hundreds of campaigns to spend them on, usually have an important constituent make the presentation.

The Art of Attending Fund-Raisers

In Washington, you can be an instant social success just by accepting all the invitations you receive to fund-raisers. Like everyone else, you'll probably be bored stiff at these gatherings. Just remember that you're not there to have fun – you're there to spend.

A friend of ours, a hugely successful lobbyist for one of the big trade associations, has to show his face at about 10 fund-raisers a month. He doesn't particularly like it, but it's a living.

This lobbyist has it down to a routine. He comes into the room, fixes a name-badge to his lapel, and grabs a glass with ice and a little soda water. (Never hard liquor – he'd be a lush if he had to hoist a glass every time someone showed him a bottle in Washington.) Glass in hand, our friend sizes up the room, smiles, and does an indigenous Washington dance called a walk-through.

He works his way around the room once, keeping a careful eye out for members of Congress or senior staffers. He banters with fellow lobbyists and he exchanges business cards with anyone he hasn't met before. Those cards don't go to the cleaners with his suit; they are carefully put onto his Rolodex the next morning. And he doesn't ever throw away the names. Today's legislative aide may be tomorrow's assistant secretary of state.

Our friend makes note of anything unusual about this party, and leaves. Elapsed time: 45 minutes. The next day, he writes a personal note to the guest of honor, saying how nice it was to hear the German band that came all the way from his district in Wisconsin to play for the guests, or to see the Tennessee clog dancers perform.

3

Finding a Congressional Sponsor

"Get a Horse!"

When you're ready to take the big step legislatively, you need a friend under the Capitol dome with access to the floor and the gymnasium. This essential person is called, rather inelegantly, a horse – a senator or representative willing to pull your wagon as your legislative champion.

Without a horse, your chances of winning are almost nil. Getting one is no cinch, however. For the member, it's not like accepting the honorary chairmanship of the Christmas Ball. Being a horse is a very difficult job at best, and a real grind when the case involves any kind of controversy.

Being a horse means a commitment to shepherding your bill through a wearing and frustrating process. It means being labeled with your cause among the media and the legislator's constituency. It means being the spokesperson, the front man, the dedicated hustler of votes among colleagues – as well as a skillful horse trader, an editorial target, and the focal point for any abuse spewed in the course of the struggle. Depending upon the intensity of the opposition, it can be a full-time job for the member and key staff, even with top-notch help from you on the research, the lobbying, the coalition building, the courting of the grassroots, and the public relations.

Targeting a congressional sponsor

To find such a paragon, scan the membership of the committee that probably will have jurisdiction over the matter. Then check the voting records of the members who sit on your side of the aisle. The possibilities will narrow quickly. When you've whittled down your choices, either try to get an introduction through your own representatives, or approach someone who is working on your side and is a constituent of the potential horse. Once you've opened the door, be sure to have chapter and verse of your case laid out and ready so the senator or representative and his staff can make an informed decision on its chances and merits. This may be the most important visit you make in Washington, so the preparation must be flawless.

The ideal horse is chairman or a senior member of the correct subcommittee who is philosophically attuned to your cause. Seniority on the committee provides extra insurance: you'll have an important advocate at every legislative stage, including a seat at the House–Senate conference at the end of the long battle, when a dedicated spokesman may be essential to keep your amendment from being dropped.

In gaining a champion, friendship goes a long way. Recognition of your name, your business, or your cause also will go a long way, as will being an employer or high official in the member's district or state. Nothing, however, will be as effective as the prospective champion's personal belief in the cause you're espousing.

Sometimes the choice will be obvious, because various members have been widely identified with certain issues: Senator Bob Packwood (R. Ore.) for the right to choice on reproductive issues, Senator Jesse Helms for the antiabortion and tobacco interests, Representative Morris K. Udall (D, Ariz.) for environmental causes, Representative Claude Pepper (D, Fla.) for senior-citizen issues, Senator James McClure (R, Ida.), for anti-gun-control matters. Each of these members believes strongly in the rightness of his cause and has proven his willingness to work for it over and over again.

Still, there are thousands of issues that do not rattle the foundations of society yet require champions. Almost always, a member of Congress will rise to propel a cause within his or her district. The issue at hand may be the building of a new dam on the east fork of a rivulet in Maine or the subsidizing of rice farms in Louisiana. In Washington the dam might be tagged pork-barrel legislation and the rice subsidy might be called a sop to the voters at the expense of a balanced budget. But that may be exactly why the voters sent a particular legislator to Washington in the first place, and reelection may hinge on the ability to deliver on that one issue. *That* creates a truly dedicated champion.

You would do well to remember that successful approaches to Congress are as much a product of tact, courtesy, and personal chemistry as they are of voter power, legal niceties, and money. In other words, it pays to be a nice person. The member of Congress who agrees to pull the wagon for your cause will give you time, commitment, prestige, legislative masterminding, staff help, and personal contact with other members. But the essential backup work of lobbying is up to you.

Case Studies: How Horses Work

Filibustering bills to death

Senator Orrin Hatch (R, Utah) will never forget his embattled position in 1977 when he was asked by the Chamber of Commerce of the United States to be the key senator fighting a Carter administration labor initiative.

A freshman on the minority side, Hatch became the legislative champion for a coalition of business interests in their struggle against the almost certain passage of a bill, introduced with the President's blessings, that gave unions more leeway in organizing, and more power in collective bargaining. The bill had won overwhelmingly in the House, and it seemed to have enough votes to pass the Senate. It was running so strong in part because the AFL-CIO had made the issue a litmus test for its friends on the Hill: "If you're our friend, you'll go to bat for us on this one." The lobbying was intense on both sides of the issue, and congressional offices were measuring their mail with yardsticks.

Hatch, a conservative, was a raw legislative rookie who ranked 98th in Senate seniority, at the bottom of the Labor and Human Resources Committee's seniority rankings. Surely, he was the least likely Republican anyone would select to take on the formidable

Democratic majority. On the other hand, recalled US Chamber of Commerce vice-president Jeffrey Joseph, "he was the only senator we could find. On its face the case was a sure loser. How were you going to beat the President of the United States, George Meany and organized labor, and the momentum created by a staggering House vote?"

Yet Hatch turned it around. When the bill came to the floor for debate before a vote that was expected to be lopsidedly for labor, Hatch reenacted *Mr Smith Goes to Washington* by staging a Senate-paralyzing filibuster that lasted five weeks. On the inside, he had the support of only a few colleagues, including fellow-Republican freshman Richard Lugar of Indiana and Democrats Ernest Hollings of South Carolina and Edward Zorinsky of Nebraska. On the outside, he had the solid backing of the US Chamber and all of its affiliates.

The filibuster was the business coalition's strategy to kill labor-law reform via Senate rules and procedures, since they couldn't lick it in a straight up-and-down vote. To get Hatch to stop talking, the Senate would have to invoke cloture, a difficult-to-pass resolution that stops all debate on a measure. Aiding Hatch was the fact that a cloture motion then required a two-thirds majority to pass. (It was reduced to three-fifths in 1979.) Although most senators despise the paralyzed condition of their chamber during a filibuster, they hate even worse making a colleague shut up. Virtually every senator can visualize an issue important enough to him to hold the floor over. The senators' innate reluctance to invoke cloture was fortified by a legion of business people, who encouraged their own senators to hold fast against shutting off debate.

The chairman of the US Chamber's support group, Robert Thompson, parked his Learjet at National Airport, just 10 minutes away from the Chamber's building, and he used it like a shuttle-bus to drop in on influential businessmen all over the country who could add that personal constituent touch to the lobbying efforts. Joseph remembers that "if Thompson phoned a likely prospect who said he was too busy, and Bob still thought he was the right person, Bob would pop into his plane and be in Arizona or Oregon that same afternoon." Few prospects could resist such a dedicated personal appeal. Meanwhile Hatch read the Bible, the phone book, and *Robert's Rules of Order* to an almost empty chamber.

While Thompson flew and Hatch orated, the business coalition got an unexpected boost. Results of a public-opinion poll commissioned by the American Retail Federation showed that a high percentage of rank-and-file union members were not in favor of labor-law reform and that the general public didn't care much for it either. The timing was perfect. Howard Baker, the Tennessee Republican who was the Senate minority leader, released the results at a press conference, and the media carried it widely.

In his five weeks on the floor of the Senate, Hatch narrowly survived six cloture votes. Finally, the bill's sponsors gave up hopes of finding the votes to break the filibuster and bring the bill to the floor. Labor-law reform was dropped. Secretariat never had a better finish than the horse from Utah.

Moving a road bill through

The filibuster that Orrin Hatch used so successfully to wear down the opposition was the garden-variety kind. Until the rules were changed recently, another way of killing a bill by talking it to death was a postcloture filibuster, a procedure that would have made even Job fidgety. When a cloture vote ended a filibuster, the defeated senator could choose to take the floor and call up lengthy printed amendments to the bill, one at a time. He could read each amendment word for word down to the last comma, and then require a roll-call vote on each one separately. In 1984 the mere threat of a postcloture filibuster helped Senator Alan Dixon (D, Ill.) to move a road bill through the Senate for his constituents.

Dixon showed up in the chamber conspicuously carrying 250 printed amendments that he stacked neatly on his desk. The Republicans, then in the majority in the Senate, huddled quickly and decided to give way because of the demands of time. Dixon won without reading a single amendment. Senators are now limited to calling up two amendments.

Horses in tandem

Two horses ran a filibuster in tandem when Warren Rudman (R, NH) and Max Baucus (D, Mont.) as a matter of principle inserted themselves prominently into a struggle that wasn't their own. They had no constituent interest in the matter – only a feeling that justice lay in a certain direction.

Alerted by a lobbyist, the two senators decided to oppose the Antitrust Contributions Act, a proposal whose outcome was of concern only to business firms found liable for violating the country's antitrust laws. The matter was of vital interest to a handful of companies, none of which had major installations in either Montana or New Hampshire.

The case – called by columnists Evans and Novak the Lobbyists' Superbowl, because the two sides used what seemed to be unlimited supplies of high-priced consulting talent – was presented to the senators as one that had to be fought over a legal principle. The bill before the Senate would allow companies that had lost price-fixing cases in court to ask Congress to overturn them years later, and to turn back the clock on the penalties as well.

Convinced that passage would interfere with the division of powers between the courts and Congress, Baucus and Rudman led a filibuster that had an unusual distinction. When the bill's proponents tried to break it, they not only failed to get the two-thirds vote needed to stop the filibuster, but the majority of the Senate sided with the filibusterers. Needless to say, the filibuster succeeded.

Standing fast for a Department of Education

Sometimes a horse wins simply by refusing to move at all. As chairman of the Senate subcommittee on education, Robert Stafford (R, Vt) stood between the Reagan administration's cost-cutting proclivities and the Department of Education, like a block of marble from his home state. Reagan wanted to eliminate the department. With most of the nation's colleges and universities depending on the gentleman from Vermont, Stafford sat at a conference table with Budget Director David Stockman and Health and Human Services Secretary Richard Schweiker and didn't give an inch.

"I'm stubborn when I know I'm right," he recalls. "I had a chance to hold out against cutting down the federal role in education, which is really not that big. We sat opposite each other one entire afternoon. Every time they came up with some new idea to beat us down, I just said no. That's one of the more pleasant memories I'll carry with me, because in the end there wasn't anything they could do about it. I hung out against them all and they had to keep the Department of Education."

Making an Oregon issue national

The perfect legislative champion is the chairman of a powerful committee who is determined to wield that power to help his or her own electorate. Senator Mark Hatfield (R. Ore.) had all those qualifications when he utilized his position as chairman of the Senate Appropriations Committee to win for his constituents a prize they had been after for more than 25 years.

The farmers of Oregon had begun to lobby for improvements on the Bonneville Lock and Dam on the Columbia River – part of the federal waterways system – in the early 1960s. Every year, some 30 million tons of agricultural cargo passed through Bonneville on the way to Pacific ports. Still, the demands of commerce in the Pacific Northwest greatly exceeded Bonneville's capacity. Planners believed that expansion of the lock would allow three times as much cargo to pass through it – an eventuality ardently desired by Oregon's farmers, and a major entry on the wish list of then Governor Mark Hatfield.

When Governor Hatfield became Senator Hatfield in 1967, he found that Bonneville wasn't the only bottleneck in the nation's waterborne commerce; it just seemed that way to impatient Oregonians. The Gallipolis Locks in West Virginia and Lock and Dam 26 on the Ohio River needed complete redevelopment. Lock and Dams 7 and 8 on the Monongahela River in Pennsylvania were impediments to any kind of orderly traffic, and the Oliver Lock on the Black Warrior River in Alabama was a relic of a sleepier era in the Old South. Many important ocean ports weren't exactly high-tech either: Baltimore was limping, and so were the Norfolk Channel and the New Orleans levee and harbor. And those were just the biggest and most pressing cases. But funding was drying up so rapidly that the US Army Corps of Engineers and the Bureau of Reclamation, the agencies that look after the waterways, had their hands full merely maintaining existing facilities.

Hatfield now saw Bonneville not just as a problem to be solved for a single state, but as a symptom of a national need. Instead of struggling for a pork-barrel appropriation for his state, he decided that Bonneville's only chance lay in treating the deteriorating infrastructure of all the waterways as a national priority.

Hatfield's big opportunity came when the Republicans took over the Senate in 1981 and he became a senior member of the leadership. As chairman of the Appropriations Committee, he turned his crusade for Bonneville into a $15 billion omnibus bill that mandated modernization of 42 other water projects across the United States. He was in the key position to get the job done, because the chairmanship of the Appropriations Committee is a post that makes everybody's list of the four most powerful positions in the Senate. (The others are the Majority Leader and the chairs of Finance, and Armed Services.)

The Appropriations Committee is charged with allocating the funds for a project after an authorizing committee establishes the need. But Hatfield took the unorthodox step of putting a laundry list of water projects into an appropriations bill without waiting for an authorizing committee to act. He admitted that this was usurpation of power, but justified his actions by pointing out that the House and Senate committees in five successive Congresses had been unable to produce such a bill.

These committees hadn't been able to forge a consensus among the competing private interests that use the nation's waterways. Also hampering their efforts were changing philosophies in the White House: Jimmy Carter had been dead set against federal payments for Western water projects. Ronald Reagan liked them but insisted on cost-sharing between federal and local authorities.

"I was one of the few Western senators who agreed with Reagan on this, and that made me a heretic," Hatfield recalls. "The others were saying that Uncle Sam, the largest landowner in most of these states, including my own, should keep up his property. I thought I was in a position to be a peacemaker, so I asked a bipartisan group of senators to get together and solve that part of the puzzle."

Cost-sharing meant that the users of the waterways would have to help defray the expense of the projects. The senator and Jeff Arnold, the staff man he assigned to hammering the bill into shape, began to scout for ideas for financing from the private interests concerned. What would fly, and what wouldn't? The backing of private interests was essential if the omnibus bill were to pass. They were the ones who would be paying the extra fees, after all. Hatfield and Arnold met with the farmers and with a seemingly endless line of shippers and carriers, and with port authorities – "Eastern ports, Gulf ports, Western ports, river ports, large ports, small ports, medium ports, Great Lakes ports, all kinds of ports, all of them with different ideas."

The senator had to create the momentum for the legislation and then keep it moving. When a bill's champion slows down, so does the bill. The various interests, intent on getting the improvements that would increase business, finally compromised on a $4-per-thousand tax on the value of all shipping in all US ports. The proceeds would go into a trust fund that would provide the 50 percent local share of the port improvement costs. The rest was up to the landlord, Uncle Sam. Similar financing methods had been used for construction of the interstate highway system and the nation's airports, so there were precedents. Congress agreed. The impetus for this nationwide series of public improvements could be traced to a bunch of Oregon farmers dreaming of expanding the Bonneville lock.

Part II

Organizing a Lobbying Campaign

one source suggests.

To have any chance of success, a lobbying campaign must have two major components that fit together like jigsaw puzzle pieces: an *inside strategy* and an *outside strategy*.

The two components require entirely different skills, and most people have neither the time nor the temperament to master both. Fortunately, lobbying needn't be a do-it-yourself endeavor. When you build your dream home in the woods, you can act as your own contractor, but you will also need the architect, the plumber, and the electrician in order to comply with the rules of the community. In lobbying, too, you need specialists, to ensure you don't get tripped up by inexperience and lack of information.

The *inside* strategy is your overall game-plan for running your case through committees in the Senate and House, through floor votes in both chambers, through a House–Senate conference, and – if you intend to launch something rather than stop something – to the Oval Office for a signing ceremony.

A bewildering array of people make a living by helping to get things accomplished in Washington. Consultants range from former secretaries of state, retired generals, and losing presidential candidates to former Nader's Raiders and specialists in the workings of only one congressional committee – the one important to you. To choose the right consultant for your project is time-consuming but worth the effort; a mistake at this point is costly. The best way to find lobbying help is through word-of-mouth, which means you have to ask for recommendations from people connected with your particular interest, profession, or business – a trade association, for example –

your elected officials on the Hill and their staffs, or your attorney back home.

Don't hesitate to interview several prospective consultants. First try the three people whose names are mentioned most to you. If you're not comfortable with any of them, talk to three more. You'll give out long before you exhaust the list of potential prospects. A high comfort-level is essential, however. You must feel certain that your Washington contact is in tune with your program.

How much does a lobbyist cost? If a great deal of money is involved in the outcome, as with an international or corporate issue in which the other side is bound to be well-financed and a tough fight is predictable, deep pockets are essential. If yours is a public interest issue, the cost could conceivably be nil or nominal, through a citizens' organization that might take up the cause and raise money to support it.

The *outside* strategy is your plan for convincing each of the lawmakers who have a voice in the outcome that his or her constituents are solidly behind your ideas. To do this, you must begin with the initial instruction of a famous English recipe for rabbit stew: "First, catch your hare." The constituents have to agree that your idea is useful to them, and they must be willing to tell their representatives just that.

The Yellow Pages are full of public relations experts, but here again, the matchup of client and consultant must be based on a successful track-record and on personal chemistry. Ask the same people who helped you locate the right lobbyist, as well as the lobbyist you just hired. When you are given a presentation, be sure to ask who will be doing the actual work of supervising and carrying out your program. Your chances of seeing the brilliant presenters very frequently once the job begins are very slim.

Warning: If any prospective consultant, inside or outside, tells you that your case is a cinch, that you are bound to win – run, don't walk, to the nearest exit. There are no cinches in Washington.

Under 10 percent of the approximately 5,000 bills introduced every year make their way into law. The average from 1975 through 1988 was about 6 percent. A truism that has made the fortunes of generations of lobbyists is that there are many more ways to stop a bill than to pass one. The House Energy and Commerce Committee, chaired by John Dingell (D, Mich.), acts on more than 10 percent of all the bills dropped in the hopper each year. But of the 626 referred to Energy and Commerce in 1987, only 22 made it through the House for consideration by the Senate.

What happened to the rest? In one way or another, they got eliminated in the race to the floor. Of the 96 that made it as far as public hearings, 39 were passed by the committee and sent to the full House. Seventeen of these died on the floor of the House. The 22 battle-scarred survivors, dealing with everything from protection against catastrophic illness to the threat of asbestos in public schools, then had to go through the same process in the Senate.

So what makes the difference? What *does* Congress respond to? John Dingell, a powerful lawmaker with 38 years in the Detroit seat that his father held before him, says that Congress moves according to a set of predictable conditions when a bill is under consideration. If you're doing business on the Hill, his basic insights should be written on every page of your appointment book and emblazoned in neon on your office wall. Here they are.

1 Congress responds to a *grassroots organization*. (*Outside*).
2 Congress responds to a *logical case*. (*Inside*).
3 Congress responds to a *lobby that speaks with one voice*. (*Inside*).
4 Congress responds to *flexibility and compromise*. (*Inside*).

These points are numbered in sequence for emphasis only. In reality, they are all played out at the same time – you can't drop one while working on the other. It helps if you can come into a congressional office with a grassroots organization waiting in the wings, because activating huge numbers of individuals and organizations takes time, and they must be ready when the logical case is being presented. Remember that the first question you'll be asked is, "Who else supports this idea?" So let's talk about the grassroots, because your opponents already have a running start on all the Dingell points and are out beating the bushes for support. You'll have to balance what they are accomplishing and then pull ahead.

4

Cultivating the Grassroots

"All Politics is Local"

If ever a statue were to be raised in Washington to former Speaker of
the House Thomas P. "Tip" O'Neill (D, Mass.), it would be
inscribed with his most memorable public comment: "All politics is
local." Those four words say it all about the grassroots. Members of
Congress are *always* aware that they represent a constituency, and
they consider *all* legislative ideas from the parochial viewpoint of,
How will it play back home? You *must* have a substantive answer
ready for that question, even though you will rarely hear it asked in
such a self-seeking form. Your answer should be based on your own
preliminary research "back home," and you should be able to reel off
the names of groups or individuals who stand behind you.

The *American Heritage Dictionary* defines *grassroots* as "people or
society at a local level rather than at the center of major political
activity." This definition is going to need some rethinking by the
editors of the next edition. With modern communications as they
are, everyone is at the center of major political activity. The Capitol
is as close as the nearest phone or the next plane. Today Mr Smith
goes to Washington at the drop of a vote he doesn't like.

On the day in March 1988 when both the Senate and the House
were deciding what to do about the President's veto of a civil
rights act, 70,000 callers, 100-to-one from angry, mobilized Reagan
supporters phoning their own legislators, crippled the Capitol's
telephone system for several hours.

The computer and the sophisticated development of the legislative support and lobbying industries in Washington have changed the grassroots from the expression of the views of a few farmers around a cracker barrel into a force of great political consequence – as well as one of America's growth industries.

The theory of grassroots cultivation is simple. It is generally true that when public opinion is behind a bill, the bill passes, and when public opinion doesn't support a bill, it doesn't pass. So if you want to convince Congress that your proposal makes the best public policy on an issue, you will have to find and motivate the voters around the country who can make your case.

The battles for the Hill in Washington, DC are won or lost on the plains of Nebraska and in the mountains of Kentucky, in the ethnic wards of Cleveland and the bays and orchards of the State of Washington. Just as it says in civics textbooks, voices from home are the most important influence on a legislator's votes.

Lobbyist Tom Korologos says amen: "The members are not going to vote this way or that way because I ask them. They are going to vote because it is good for the district – which means it is good for them. Your job as a lobbyist is to find out what is good for them back home and to identify why this is a good vote politically."

A member of Congress would rather see one voter than 10 lobbyists. This is known as the Plant Manager Theory of Lobbying. Send the regional plant manager into Washington on Wednesday to meet with his congressman or one of the state's senators to explain the company position on giving 60 days' notice on plant closings, and he'll get an appointment. Even a freshman legislator knows that if he doesn't meet with *this* voter – even though he has the flu, his wife is delivering their first child, and the President has invited him to lunch – by next Tuesday a lot of voters in his district are going to hear about the airs their congressman is putting on now that he's living in Washington.

Sometimes, nothing beats a few minutes face to face with the member for delivering a message. Lynn Greenwalt, vice-president of the National Wildlife Federation, masterminds the mailing of millions of letters per year to activate his environmentally protective membership. He keeps the cards, phone calls, and Mailgrams pouring into congressional offices.

"But when the real crunch comes," Greenwalt notes, "we ask one of our supporters – say, a trout fisherman who is concerned about the acid rain and industrial effluent ruining his trout stream – to make a trip to Washington. We will almost always use one person in a key congressional district who knows what he is talking about and has an interest in keeping the environment wholesome – not just for humans but all other creatures as well. That gives you a lobbyist who is believable. Grassroots comes in all sizes, from mass to individual."

One of your jobs is to make sure that whoever is representing the grassroots has been briefed thoroughly before the encounter with the legislator. Representative Sam Gibbons (D, Fla.), a key figure in the House as chairman of the Trade Subcommittee, tells the sad story of the businessman-constituent whose trade association had made an urgent appointment for him. He bustled in, settled into the leather chair in Gibbons's private office, exchanged pleasantries, and then fell silent. Finally, he burst out, "Sam, they told me I had to drop everything and come up here and see you immediately, but I'm damned if I know what we're supposed to talk about."

Oregon Senator Bob Packwood, ranking Republican on the Senate Finance Committee, has occasionally wondered whether there is any real purpose behind the visits of some delegations. "They arrive on time for appointments that they made weeks in advance through their organization's Washington representatives. They make themselves comfortable. We have very pleasant cocktail-party type conversations, and they leave after a half-hour looking very gratified. Which, of course, pleases me. But if there was a purpose to this encounter beyond the civilities, I never learned it."

So attuned are members of the House and Senate to local issues that Congress consistently has trouble passing foreign-aid bills, because few voters care much about big international issues. Hearings on world trouble spots such as Angola produce eye-glaze in the public from Maine to Arizona. Few people have a personal interest in a country they can't even find on a globe. But foreign problems that affect particular regions of the country – such as immigration in Texas and California – or touch the ethnic heritage of some Americans – such as those involving Israel, Ireland, Italy (the celebrated Three I League for mandatory overseas visits by urban politicians) and Greece – are a different story. Partisan constituencies are always alert to keeping legislators in line on their issues.

Central America, for example, is an area close to home for Texans and Floridians, so its problems draw the attention of those state's delegations to Washington. When a politician gives a speech decrying the presence of "Communism at our doorsteps" and asking for support for the Contras, Dallas and Miami will take the threat personally and respond with grassroots support. To Detroit and Des Moines, Nicaragua might just as well be Angola.

Jimmy Carter managed to make an international issue into a local farm issue when he punished the Russians for invading Afghanistan by canceling wheat sales to the Soviet Union and thereby hitting American farmers right in the pocketbook. Carter's sanctions hurt Moscow, Idaho, more than they hurt Moscow, USSR, because the Commissar had the nerve to act like the customer he was: he put his order for wheat on the world market, and the Soviets bought from Argentina and Canada instead of the United States. The farmers bombarded Congress, and the repercussions went on for six years, long after Carter had gone back to Georgia.

Because voices from home are much more audible in chorus, millions of Americans join together under one banner or another to let Congress know, loudly and clearly, how they want to be represented on the issues. The reflexive response of the legislature to organized groups leaves senators such as Utah's Jake Garn wondering whether he is doing justice to the unorganized. At every hearing while he was chairman of the Senate Banking, Housing, and Urban Affairs Committee, Garn tried to ferret out an unaffiliated banker or farmer or real-estate agent who might possibly represent himself as a citizen, voter, family man, and working adult rather than as the representative of committee, coalition, association, or union.

Grassroots movements transcend political parties. Americans may label themselves Republicans or Democrats, but they are far more committed and active when they are bonded by a need, a belief, or a cause. The individuals who join together to force the hand of Congress are the Minutemen of our day. The millions of men and women who made their legislators retreat in 1982 on a bill to collect income taxes on interest and dividends at the source were rich and poor, black and white, old and young. All they had in common were savings accounts or shares in publicly held companies. And the most powerful standing grassroots lobbies, such as the American Association of Retired Persons, make a fetish out of insisting that they care nothing for politics, just for issues.

Members of Congress of all stripes receive instructions from voters of all stripes. Often the instructions come neatly packaged in Mailgrams and letters orchestrated by lobbying groups or through the powerful prime-time TV forum available to the President of the United States. President Reagan made Western Union rich during his eight years of effectively urging the voters to communicate with their congressional representatives *now*, right from their living rooms. And letters still arrive, neatly scripted or scrawled by individuals who decided on their own to tell their representative what's on their minds.

The system clearly favors the organized. A stream of letters prompted by the National Rifle Association will certainly make one viewpoint highly visible and leave clear hints of reelection problems ahead for the wrong vote. Communications are instantaneous, both to Congress and to the lobby memberships. The Washington representatives carefully watch the absentee records and the character of the votes of the officials, and the word goes forth around the country who in Congress is good and who is bad.

Speaker of the House Jim Wright says that mail from home (Fort Worth, Texas) is a barometer – not necessarily of how the public would respond in a Gallup poll or a Harris poll, but of the intensity of feeling on one side or another: "A question may be divided about 50–50 in the public's mind, but if one side is lackadaisical and not motivated to tell the member of Congress how they feel, the mail will tilt more than five to one to the activist side – those who are fired up and enthused and adamant in their positions." Wright adds that the weight of this mail unquestionably exerts a subliminal effect on the member. "If people feel strongly enough about an issue to write to you, then quite likely they will feel strongly enough about it to vote for or against you on the basis of how you respond."

Representative John Dingell maintains that the House is more responsive to citizen action than the Senate because "the districts are smaller; representatives have more intimate acquaintance with the people they serve. Their terms are shorter, so they are at home more frequently."

The grassroots outpouring least likely to be effective comes in the form of laundry-list petitions with long columns of names. According to Jim Wright, "Those of us who have been here for a while are fairly adept at distinguishing genuine interest from artificially generated pressure. As a group, members of Congress are probably more influenced by 10 or 12 well-written, obviously sincere and personal letters than we would be by 1,000 names on a petition."

In the course of their legislative duties, members often make widespread use of the grassroots networks to sway the votes of their colleagues. Nothing beats a voice from home. Bob Michel, Republican leader of the House, credits the help he got from Washington trade associations with running up the winning margin when he was the point-man in the House for President Reagan's 1981 tax-reduction bill. Urgently needing votes in the House to score a victory for the President, Michel leaned on all the members he could influence and collected years of IOUs for favors done. When the chips were down, however, he cast about for a way to apply constituent pressure. He brought the problem to the national trade associations in Washington, asking for their help in reaching a list of members whose votes might be undecided or wavering.

"We were 53 votes behind, and we worked out a combination with the Southern Democrats who came to be known as the Boll Weevils. But it was touch-and-go, and a very important force out there was the associations. There isn't a district in the US that isn't touched by their memberships. When you get that one-to-one contact with a member of Congress from someone important to him in his district, and you get that double-checked by several other groups coming at him from diverse angles, then you're getting close to a firm commitment on a vote."

Similarly, Representative Morris K. Udall, chairman of the House Interior and Insular Affairs Committee, convened regular meetings of cosponsors and supporters of his Alaska Lands bill when it was ready for a floor fight. The only item on the agenda at these sessions was going over lists of House members who might be persuaded to vote the right way and lists of those people back home who were good candidates to do the persuading.

Chairman Udall was looking for ways to apply g. assroots muscle to his colleagues. Even if it is a matter of winning over a close friend in the House or Senate, a member often will prefer to stir up some interest in the friend's backyard and have the approach come from a supporter in Indiana or Oregon than from a source in Washington.

"I don't want to hear it from you," growled Representative Charles Rangel (D, NY) to a public relations consultant in 1984. "I want to hear from New York charities how great and important the Altman Foundation is to them. That's what counts." Rangel had agreed to sponsor a bill giving the 70-year-old foundation, created by one of New York's merchant princes, more time to divest itself of the B. Altman stores, as required by a tax law. Before the week was out, he was provided with a list of blue-ribbon institutions, including the Salvation Army, the Boy Scouts and Girl Scouts, St Luke's Hospital, and Catholic, Jewish, and Protestant welfare organizations – some of which had been receiving checks from the foundation every year since 1919. A civic luncheon sponsored by the foundation with the Metropolitan Museum of Art, the other major recipient of Benjamin Altman's largesse – he had transformed it overnight into a world-class museum by willing it, among other treasures, his 13 Rembrandts – resulted in a favorable editorial in the New York *Daily News*. Among the millions of New Yorkers reading the *News* that day was Senator Daniel Patrick Moynihan (D, NY), who became the bill's sponsor in the Senate.

Organizing the Grassroots

Despite the high-tech nature of many grassroots campaigns, individual ingenuity is still needed to do the job right. Support can be found wherever the people are found – in stores, churches, athletic arenas, even in the waiting rooms of doctors' offices. Thus, when the Planned Parenthood Federation of America had to battle proposed legislation that would have diminished federal funding for family planning, each of the 190 Planned Parenthood clinics became a center of communications to Congress.

The proposal was to change the way federal funds were distributed for family welfare. The Reagan administration's plan was to deliver the money in block grants to the state governments rather than deliver it directly to hospitals and clinics that were engaged in family planning and pregnancy counseling. If the PPFA had to depend upon funding by the states, rather than the federal government, the clinics would be threatened with near extinction.

The Federation feared that state governments might divert block grants away from controversial family planning needs to such politically popular projects as building swimming pools in middle-class districts.

So the organization urged patients to fight back by writing letters. While waiting to see a doctor or nurse, the women were provided with paper, pen, envelopes and stamps, and a short printed note explaining why their help was needed.

Some 50,000 such letters hit Washington. These were real letters signed personally by real people with real addresses. Who would fail to be moved by a letter like the following?:

> Senator:
> I am 20 years old and I work as a waitress in a small restaurant here. I get minimum wage and tips, but I have no health insurance and there is no money for a doctor. If the Planned Parenthood clinic here is closed, I will have nowhere to go for health care or for advice.
>
> Sincerely.

Such missives provided the ammunition needed by Senator Bob Packwood of Oregon, who bucked his Republican leadership to lead a bipartisan group that managed to retain federal funding for Planned Parenthood, although at a reduced rate.

PPFA's patients made up an ad hoc group that conducted only one quick in-and-out legislative thrust and then disbanded. Many other Americans are organized for continuing political action through their professions, trades, or social or political clubs. At a call from their modern-day Paul Revere, the Washington lobbyist, groups of real-estate agents, morticians, teachers, blue-collar workers, veterans, bird watchers, gun owners, pacifists, senior citizens, and citizens in hundreds of other categories begin to move. They may be asked to deluge Congress with letters, cards, phone calls, Mailgrams, and personal visits. Or they may be asked to concentrate heavy volleys on a representative who is undecided on the issue, or who needs a display of support from the voters back home to justify her position.

Lists of people likely to be interested in a piece of legislation are generated by computer according to the magazines they subscribe to, the churches they attend, their line of work, their neighborhoods, their clubs and fraternal organizations, the charities they support. Letters are churned out by the million, addressing them by name and asking them to stand up and be counted for the cause. And if individual citizens don't want to be bothered with writing a letter, hunting for a stamp, and finding a mailbox, the organizers of the cause are more than willing to do it for them. When the mail is handled centrally, the organizers *know* that the voice of the people will be delivered in impressive numbers and in the right place at the right time.

Richard Viguerie, a direct-mail wizard for conservative causes, sends 102 million letters a year to lists that represent, to a large extent, single-issue voters on the right. Roger Craver, Viguerie's counterpart on the left, mails an equal number to voters whose sympathies run to liberal causes. Both use the letters to raise funds and to stimulate mailings to the Hill for issues they represent. They both count on a 10 percent success rate on letters to the Hill – which translates into another 20 million letters for the Capitol mailmen every year. Letters asking for money generate about a 3 percent return, which provides enough cash to keep the next batch of letters moving.

If letters and Mailgrams and phone calls are not enough, a lobbyist will ask the grassroots group to fan out personally on the Hill, visiting members individually to make the case for support for their issue. Early in 1988, for example, the nation's independent insurance agents turned out in impressive numbers to protect the insurance business from invasion by the banks. More than 700 agents spread over the Hill, selling public policy rather than insurance policies. Their strength as a significant grassroots force lay in numbers – they represented some 125,000 agents from coast to coast, prominent in small towns and big cities, and they were well connected. The delegation included the brothers of two Democratic senators, George Mitchell of Maine, and Daniel K. Inouye of Hawaii, who had no problems with sibling rivalry on this issue. Impressed by the outpouring, Senator William Proxmire (D, Wis.), then chairman of the Banking Committee, told *The New York Times*, "There are more insurance agents in New Jersey alone than there are banks in the whole country." The agents prevailed.

All successful Grassroots Campaigns have in Common . . .
1   A cause that substantial numbers of people can rally around.
2   Access to lists of voters likely to be interested in the success of the cause.
3   A Washington connection to supply current legislative information and advise on strategy and tactics. ·
4   An education campaign aimed at keeping the supporters informed and willing to act.
5   A concentrated effort to get the views of the voters to the Hill in timely fashion.
6   A cadre of members of Congress who are ideologically attuned to the issue and see substantial support for it in their districts.

Starting a Grassroots Organization

One of the most graphic illustrations of how to get a grassroots organization started came from that great Tammany Hall politician George Washington Plunkitt (who became famous for rationalizing a distinction between "honest graft" and "dishonest graft"). Plunkitt began his career in the 1880s by corraling the one voter he could count on, his cousin Tommy. He followed through by adding the young men on his floor of a boardinghouse, then those in the entire building, then those on the block. Soon he had gained a voice in the party as a person who controlled some votes.

The situation isn't too different today. You can start a grassroots organization simply by recruiting a few like-minded friends or associates who are willing to work and be visible on an issue that concerns all of you.

That's exactly how a group of unhappy businessmen from Muskogee, Oklahoma, turned around a bankruptcy law that they found inequitable. The law, passed by Congress in 1983, supposedly gave a fair shake to debtors in bankruptcy proceedings. Claiming that the new law contained loopholes large enough to drive an unpaid Cadillac through, the businessmen approached the local office of their Democratic congressman, Rep. Mike Synar, asking for an appointment to show why they needed redress.

As a majority member of the House Judiciary Committee, which deals with bankruptcy legislation, Synar had been active in fashioning the law. He thought it was fair as written, so he wasn't inclined to give high priority to complaints about it. Still, a congressman slights his constituents at his peril, so Synar scheduled a meeting – at 7.00 AM at the airport in Muskogee, just before his plane was to take off for Washington.

When he arrived at the airport, Synar found a crowd of 170 prominent local merchants – bankers, department store executives, finance-company and credit-union officers, and auto dealers. They had been organized for this pre-breakfast initiative by the Washington lobbyist for the national coalition fighting for change in the bankruptcy law. In an effort to get Synar's support for that change, they told him firsthand stories about flaws that were allowing many customers to declare bankruptcy and still keep merchandise they had purchased on credit.

Surprised by the large turnout, as well as by the stories of the law's negative economic impact on his district, Synar changed his mind. He sponsored a revision of the bankruptcy act, and it sailed through the House with 285 cosponsors.

The Muskogee businessmen managed to *localize a national problem* successfully. A variation on this same principle was applied by the American Medical Association when it managed to personalize a proposed federal law that was a national pocketbook issue for the medical profession. This campaign began when the AMA lobbyist in Washington alerted his membership of the impending passage of a bill that would place a cap on fees paid to physicians for certain services under Medicare.

Representative Dan Rostenkowski, the Chicago Democrat who chairs the House Ways and Means committee and thus must constantly come up with new ways to finance the government, thought he had the votes for this bill in the bag and the money as good as in the Treasury. The cap would save millions in fees and concern only a relatively small number of voters who were, in any case, generally affluent. But the chairman hadn't counted on the power of the family doctor.

Physicians around the country resorted to the ultimate weapon of their profession: the House call. They visited selected members of the House of Representatives – in particular, those who served with Rostenkowski on Ways and Means. The doctors were able to convince their members of Congress that cutting fees was a bad idea whose time had not come, and the chairman was unable to swing a majority vote for the proposal.

Case Studies: Bucking the Establishment

Common Cause gets underway

Occasionally, it's possible to hit up the rich and powerful for money to build a lobbying group that will benefit ordinary citizens who are otherwise underrepresented. That's what happened in the case of Common Cause.

Common Cause grew out of the National Urban Coalition, which was founded after the ghetto riots of 1968. Created by the Establishment, the NUC was made up of corporation executives, powerful mayors, union leaders, and leaders of black militant groups, and was headed by John Gardner, a former Johnson Administration cabinet member who was a patrician to his toes. Gardner and the people who backed him thought that a broad-based coalition offered a way to lobby successfully for legislation that would strengthen civil rights and the communities that had been torn apart by the riots.

It was a great idea, but it didn't work. The Urban Coalition was getting $4 million a year from foundations, but tax laws prevented it from doing any lobbying. To circumvent this roadblock, a splinter group, the Urban Coalition Action Council, was created as the organization's lobbying arm. Because the latter was financed with nondeductible dollars, however, it was constantly struggling to raise money. In the rare instances that the Action Council managed to win a legislative victory, the battle would alienate some of the sponsors. Often, its legislative efforts were blocked by the conservative Southern Democrats who ran all the powerful committees at the time.

At this point, Gardner and his associates concluded that they still didn't have the right organization in the field. They wanted a broad-based constituency of citizens that could change the way Congress was run. Gardner's advisers, Tom Mathews and Roger Craver, thought they could build that constituency with the new direct-mail techniques (this was 1970). The problem was how to reach and build that constituency.

Fortunately, Gardner had a number of rich friends who supported his ideas. Before joining the Cabinet, he had been head of the Carnegie Foundation, where he had access to people such as Douglas Dillon, Averell Harriman, and the Rockefellers. From these and other friends, he collected $250,000 to start his grassroots citizens group. (In 1989, it would have cost more than $1 million.)

Working with direct-mail writers in San Francisco and the Doyle Dane Bernbach ad agency in New York, Mathews came up with an advertising campaign. They agreed on a name, Common Cause, and a slogan, "Everyone's Organized but the People." They took out ads in the major newspapers and started a direct-mail campaign. Success came immediately.

The ad in *The New York Times* cost $15,000 and returned $100,000 in contributions – an amazing feat in light of the fact that such an ad usually breaks even. Direct-mail contributions were running two to three times the rate for a typical campaign.

In six months, Common Cause had 100,000 members and $1.5 million in the bank. Within three years, it had 325,000 members and $8 million-more money than the Democratic Party had at that point. And the demographic characteristics of the members were a lobbyist's dream: older, educated, community leaders, all of them politically aware. Congressmen and senators found that they couldn't ignore Common Cause. During the Watergate scandals, the group was a persistent gadfly, filing lawsuits against the Committee to Re-Elect the President (CREEP) that forced the release of lists of illegal corporate campaign contributions running into millions of dollars.

Fortified by that kind of clout, Common Cause got solidly behind the congressional reformers of the class of 1974. By using seed money from the very rich, Common Cause built a remarkably effective grassroots organization.

Starting the Conservative Caucus

At the other end of the political spectrum from Common Cause lies the Conservative Caucus, which has 400,000 members nationwide. It was founded in 1974 as an organizational rallying point for opponents of the Panama Canal Treaty by Howard Phillips and Richard Viguerie, who knew that for millions of Americans the Canal was an emotional symbol of US strength and resolve – not to mention sovereignty over the Atlantic and Pacific oceans. The proposed treaty, which gave the canal to Panama at the end of the century, was considered by these citizens to be an act of betrayal against their children and grandchildren.

"We found that there were many more of us than we had really anticipated," Viguerie recalls. "We had no lists – we had to compile them. We took them from people who subscribed to magazines that had the defense of the country at heart. We copied the names on the lists of Goldwater campaign contributors. We also got names from our supporters who knew other people they thought could be recruited. We worked very much on a South and West geographic distribution, because after all, the Panama Canal is much more real to people in the Southwest than it is to people in Maine."

When the treaty was finally ratified in 1978, Phillips and Viguerie kept the Panama Canal treaty dissenters together. They had found a significant corps of people willing to make a stand and put up money to fight for issues ranging from Right-to-Life to a hands-off policy on South Africa. Phillips feels that many decisions that have come out of Congress on anticommunist foreign policy can be traced to the work done by Conservative Caucus volunteers who wrote, phoned, and visited their representatives. They were on the phones in favor of helping the Nicaragua Contras, opposing aid to Mozambique, and opposing sanctions against South Africa.

All these causes depend for financing on arousal of the public through national visibility. Viguerie said that his letters had almost a 50 percent response on South Africa, primarily because the issue was being discussed in headlines and news broadcasts day after day. "We get much more success with issues that are in the headlines," he claims.

Phillips's first post-treaty order of business was to see that those who had voted to "give away" the Panama Canal would not be returned to office in the 1980 election. His clout was formidable. The Conservative Caucus campaigned across the country, and Phillips believes that its negative efforts contributed to the defeat of 13 senators and representatives.

He has also notched his belt with victories in other right-wing concerns. The Caucus was active in the defeats of the Equal Rights Amendment and of the constitutional amendment to grant statehood to the District of Columbia.

Phillips and Viguerie claim they never speak directly to a representative or a senator; instead, they rely on mobilizing citizens to write to legislators and to contribute money to conservative causes. Members of Congress are invited to speak at the Caucus's national meetings and training workshops, however.

The stories behind Common Cause and the Conservative Caucus may represent the most remarkable instances of building grassroots clout on a string of addresses, but they are by no means the only ones. Common Cause inspired TV producer Norman Lear to put some of the money he made from *All in the Family* behind another liberal grassroots group, People for the American Way, which has staked out an agenda based on civil rights and legal issues. Ralph Nader parlayed his status as a highly publicized fighter for consumer safety into a grassroots conglomerate called Public Citizen, whose divisions match Nader's conception of the nation's dangers – nutrition, environment, legal matters, and product safety.

All of these organizations use absolutely parallel approaches to their work. They *stake out a position.* They *find specific groups of people likely to be sympathetic to that position.* And then they *stimulate a grassroots campaign to support it.*

The grassroots endeavors carried out by Washington activist David Cohen on defense issues follow these steps implicitly.

Cohen takes on the Establishment

David Cohen has been successfully butting his head against the Establishment – defined in his case as the military–industrial complex and every administration – for the last 20 years. His win–loss record is remarkable. As an activist, he came up through the Vietnam War protests and the presidency of Common Cause.

During the Reagan era, Cohen devoted himself to fighting the administration on its principal nuclear defense proposals – first the MX missile, and then the "Star Wars" strategic defense initiative.

Cohen conducts his activities under the shingle of the Professionals' Coalition for Nuclear Arms Control, which includes such highly educated groups as the Union of Concerned Scientists, Physicians for Social Responsibility, Lawyers' Alliance for Nuclear Arms Control, and Architects, Designers, and Planners for Social Responsibility – all of which are supported by voluntary contributions from members. These organizations are made up principally of bright young academics who are willing to give the time and effort to political action on issues of conscience. Because of their special skills in the sciences, they are able to lobby their legislators with an unusual combination of expertise and grassroots concern.

As the quarterback for a coalition of very individual personalities, Cohen merely calls the plays and passes the ball to the players for the actual lobbying. He perceives his mission as "getting more participants at the table" in public-policy decisions. He even runs postgraduate lobbying courses for amateurs at a nonprofit center, the Advocacy Institute, which he operates with Michael Pertschuk, chairman of the Federal Trade Commission in the Carter administration.

Because public interest lobbyists do not have the financial resources of industry or labor representatives, Cohen must be an opportunist who makes the most of every chance he gets.

"A public interest lobbyist must think in strategic terms, in entrepreneurial terms," he says. "The biggest challenge is how to make a meeting with a congressman interesting and memorable to the congressman. How do you show him that a lot of people care? We're always looking for something that works in one place that can be used around the country."

Once when a Cohen associate phoned the Washington office of a key swing-vote congressman, she discovered that her quarry was back in his district office, taking calls from constituents. Sitting in her own Washington office, she arranged to be a guest on a radio call-in program in the congressman's home town. On the air, she told her listeners that if they cared about the issue, they could reach the congressman directly, right then, for the cost of a local phone call. The response was a flood of phone calls to the member, who was thus alerted that the issue was important to the people who elected him.

The arms-control issues that take up Cohen's time are never decided by a single roll-call vote. They go on and on. Because Cohen and his colleagues are pragmatists, they always begin preparing for the next vote the minute the previous one has been counted.

"We have to be content the first time around with losing but knowing that we have brought the issue into the public eye," he says. "Our job is to create conflict, to create controversy, to divide Congress into pros, cons, and the undecided. The vote tells us who our strongest supporters are, who our opponents are, and who is in the middle. Then we're ready to go to work on the next vote."

In dealing with nuclear weapons, Cohen knows he will always be up against well-prepared Pentagon generals backed by defense contractors with a stake in the outcome. His counter-strategy is to present a member of Congress with an articulate, well-informed, and sincere scientist who votes in his district, and let the two of them talk the issue over.

On the tough public issues, Cohen says, scientist- and physician-constituents are credible even when they are expounding on subjects outside their fields of expertise. And, he says, the best place to get the scientist and the member together is not at the congressional offices in Washington, but at an informal occasion back home in the district, where there's time enough to chat: "The legislator can see that our people know what they are talking about, and that they can't be bamboozled. Legislators respond more positively on this kind of issue to people – real people – who are well-informed but don't work for a manufacturer."

Volunteer lobbyists are most effective with Congress when they have one burning issue, philosophical or financial, to fight for. All they need is someone to organize them and point the way.

5

Mobilizing the Grassroots for Business Issues

American business has learned that it needs voices from the hinterlands – employees, shareholders, suppliers, customers – to win on the Hill.

Marshaling the Voices of Customers

Price is a powerful stimulant for rousing customers into expressing themselves on issues before Congress. During the height of legislative activity on the omnibus trade bill in 1986 and 1987, stores that depend heavily on imports enlisted the help of their customers in trying to stave off protectionism. Sign-up desks near the checkout counters of discount department stores minced no words in recruiting grassroots support. "Tell Congress you don't want higher prices!" commanded one sign in an Arlington, Virginia store, which supplied postcards addressed to the area's officials.

When the insurance industry was opposing legislation mandating gender-neutral life-insurance policies, a proposal supported by feminist groups, the insurers conducted a skillful mail effort addressed to women policyholders. Of course there were male policy rates and female policy rates, they wrote, but the actuarial tables favored the women. The clincher was that women were paying less for coverage than men and that unisex insurance would only cause their premiums to go up. The policyholders were urged to let their members of Congress know that they didn't want higher insurance rates. They did, and the issue faded fast.

When credit card companies wanted to fight a proposed sur-charge on charge purchases that would make buying with plastic more expensive than paying cash, the company knew just where to go for supporters. Along with monthly statements, they distributed postcards of complaint that customers could send to their represent-atives. Senator Alan Dixon (D, Ill.) alone received 100,000 of these cards in three weeks. As a result, despite a formidable lobby in favor of surcharges – including the National Retail Merchants Association, the Consumer Federation of America, and the Service Station Dealers of America – Congress extended the law making it illegal to charge more for a credit-card purchase than for a cash transaction.

The grassroots categories in these cases were well-established groups – women and shoppers – that could easily be identified as legitimate voices on the Hill. There was an undiscovered world to conquer, however, when the Home Recording Rights Coalition lobbyists started out to protect the videocassette recorder (VCR) manufacturers from incursions on their profits by the motion picture and television industries.

How video stores became politicized

Lobbyist James O'Hara knew that he wasn't involved in an ordinary legislative battle when Senator Paul Laxalt (R, Nev.) listened politely to his case and then asked, "What does Wayne Newton think of this?" Wayne Newton's opinion is not normally a weather vane for Washington policy, but in this case it meant a lot to the Nevada senator: the Las Vegas singer was an important constituent and campaign supporter of the senator's, and O'Hara was lobbying on an entertainment issue.

O'Hara's clients were the Sony Corporation and other manufacturers of VCRs, who were fighting a battle that had spilled over into Congress from a series of judicial actions culminating in a Supreme Court decision. When Sony in 1976 started to talk about marketing its new Betamax home-recording device, Gary Shapiro, legal counsel to the Electronic Industries Association, voiced concern about possible copyright infringements. Justifying his concerns, the movie industry filed a lawsuit the same year, charging that VCR owners would, in essence, pirate copyrighted material.

After a US district court ruled against them, the motion picture people, with a big financial stake in the outcome, appealed, and in October 1981 a federal circuit court reversed the decision. The opinion of the circuit-court judges was that the copyrights of the movie-makers were indeed being infringed, because movies were being taped off TV sets and shown again without permission. The court said responsibility for this copyright infringement lay with the VCR manufacturers and their advertising agencies.

Within three days of the decision, three unrelated bills were introduced in Congress to make home recording legal. The electronics industry, recovering rapidly from a state of shock, began to prepare the Supreme Court appeal they would eventually win. In the meantime, however, its allies would have to find a grassroots constituency, fast. They did, and the unexpected but amazingly effective help they found all around the country seemed to come right out of the script of a Frank Capra movie.

After deciding to form a coalition, the manufacturers had to come up with a name for it. Initially they settled on the Right to Tape Coalition. That name didn't survive very long, however, because it contained two connotations considered negative inside the Beltway: only a few years after Nixon and Watergate, "taping" was thought to have a sinister ring to it; and "right to tape" sounded too much like "right to life." So they came up with Home Recording Rights Coalition.

Their plan was to support aggressively House bills already introduced by Representatives Tom Foley (D, Wash.) and Stan Parris (R, Va.). That support included help to be recruited from retailers and consumers. The National Retail Merchants Association pitched in, as did the National Association of Retail Dealers.

Hearings were held within a few weeks on a pro-Hollywood bill introduced by Senator Charles Mathias (R, Md.), which gave the manufacturers' coalition the good fortune to hear and see – live and in person – the case Hollywood had prepared for Congress. Congress is as star-struck as the rest of the nation, so the opportunity to have a double feature with appearances by Charlton Heston and Clint Eastwood made for a big day on the Hill. But the romance is deeper than tinsel, because Hollywood stars and executives are among the most effective of fund-raisers for many members of Congress. An appearance by a film star at a congressional fund-raiser is a proven draw for both people and money. Also, the Motion Picture

Association of America is a prestigious social presence in Washington, with its elegant screening-room for new movies and its short list of prominent guests.

A major movie executive testified before Mathias's Judiciary subcommittee that the new video recorders presented a threat to the movies and that a royalty of $50 per machine should be levied on VCRs. At that time, with VCRs still a novelty, the fee would have amounted to no more than $10 million per year. No one, not Sony or Matsushita or the Hollywood producers, really expected the movie rental business to grow into the vast industry it is today. The principal uses for VCRs at that time were for home showing of what are euphemistically called adult movies and for the then newly developing American sport of time-shifting – recording the football games for later viewing, for example.

Shapiro and other experts felt that the one-time tax could have been enacted without eliciting a heavy challenge from the industry. After all, the tax would have been charged directly to the consumer, who was apparently ready to buy the product at any price.

But Mathias's legislation set up an entire procedure on copyright protection, thus complicating an essentially simple matter. Besides authorizing a royalty, the bill gave the copyright owners (the film-makers) the right to control the distribution of the tapes. This meant that a video dealer would need Hollywood's permission to rent out a videotape of a movie.

At this time the rental market was just starting to emerge. Originally, video stores had tried to *sell* tapes of movies. Strong buyer resistance, however, led to the proliferation of rentals. The film-makers, of course, would have preferred to sell everyone copies of their movies at $70 to $80. But if the market favored rentals, Mathias's bill would at least give them a slice of the rental fees plus control of the distribution right down to the consumer's living room.

When the significance of that provision became apparent – namely, that the renting of movies would be expensive for the viewer and much less profitable for the video dealers – the electronics industry found itself with an opportunity for a grassroots campaign. The as-yet unorganized video dealers could be roused to protect their fledgling businesses.

"It was such a fuzzy market that we didn't even know at that time that video rentals in the stores were contributing to the sales of

VCRs," recalls Shapiro. "Trying to get a piece of the rental market was Hollywood's biggest legislative mistake."

The manufacturers formed an alliance with the video dealers. Shapiro and others went around the country to visit individually with the 200 or so dealers and help organize them into a trade association. Simultaneously, public relations counselor John Adams was assigned to fan a grassroots fire. Adams and his associate, Jack Bonner, were acting on a theory spun out by Tommy Boggs, O'Hara's partner and chief lobbyist for the Home Recording Rights Coalition.

Boggs reasoned that in practical grassroots terms, the movie industry has a very slight sway over Congress except in Southern California and New York City, where it is a major employer. His objective was to generate visible opposition from video dealers and their customers in as many congressional districts as possible, in an effort to outweigh the glamour and the fund-raising effectiveness that movie stars and directors brought to Washington.

Bonner, who had worked on the Hill for Senator John Heinz (R, Pa.), observed that Hollywood's power in Congress was so compelling that even normally proconsumer senators such as Ted Kennedy were committed to the other side. "I said, 'Why don't we stop talking about royalty fees and copyright laws and call this thing a tax? That will help people understand what we're talking about'."

Organizing the video dealers took extraordinary patience, because the dealers usually were completely apolitical. Many were mechanics or factory workers who had suddenly turned retailer, and their minds were on customers, deliveries, the bookkeeper, and a hundred other details.

"I was calling about this big problem in Washington and the dealer's big problems were, 'Is the inventory all right? Did the salesman show up? Am I pricing everything right?' I'd be in the middle of my big pitch and he'd have to wait on a customer and I'd hang on till he got back. We had to make it easy for him to get involved."

The video dealers and the stores that sold VCRs were asked to put up counter cards containing petitions to be signed by the customers. As the responses poured in by the thousands, the names were verified by the public relations firm and affixed to Mailgrams addressed to representatives and senators.

The next step was to arrange meetings for legislators back in their districts – preferably in the video stores, where they could personally hear the voices of their constituents. If the member couldn't get back home, conference calls were arranged from the district to Washington.

Bonner explains the appeal of the approach: "I've spent my life in politics, and there is nothing more effective than a constituent looking a member right in the eye and saying, 'Senator, I have my life's work invested in this business. If you vote for this you're going to cause serious problems for me and my customers. I don't know politics, but people are renting movies from me because I give good value for the dollar. Please don't mess me up in favor of some people who live in Hollywood and don't live or vote in Tucson.'"

The Hill listened. When the West Virginia Mailgrams hit the office of Senator Robert Byrd, outlining the problem and inviting him to a meeting back in the state, the senator himself telephoned the first three people on the list for verification. Satisfied that all three were aware of the Mailgrams and actually knew something about the issue, Byrd telephoned the coalition's headquarters to say that although he couldn't get back home for a meeting he would be delighted if five West Virginians could come and have lunch with him in his private office. The carefully selected delegation included a person from the West Virginia Consumer Federation, a mine worker, and a video retailer.

The real value of the luncheon was that none of the people questioned by the senator said, "I don't remember signing that" or "I don't feel that way about it." "That would have poisoned every letter we sent up there," Bonner said. "The senator would have mentioned the incident to other senators and before you know it, the whole thing would have been contaminated. Quality control made a difference."

Public opinion was swamping Hollywood's boat very quickly. Representative Dan Glickman (D, Kan.), who as head of the Congressional Arts Caucus had agreed to cosponsor the Hollywood version of the video bill, changed his mind when 1,000 Mailgrams landed on his desk. He told a reporter, "It's a perfect example of learning what the people want and knowing that's what you're here to represent."

The West Virginia group never got the chance to find out if their lunch with Senator Byrd had won a supporter for tax-free video rental, because the issue never came to a vote in the Senate. On the day Senator Mathias had chosen for the subcommittee to vote, five of its seven members were coincidentally unable to attend. All had been lobbied by members of the coalition. Lacking a quorum, Mathias dropped the subject.

Hollywood had lost the round and decided to withdraw – at least for the moment.

Toshiba comes from behind

The most unusual rallying of the grassroots in recent years came in the unexpected and powerful lobbying by American big business to overturn sanctions voted by the Senate against the Toshiba Corporation, a major Japanese competitor, in 1987. Companies such as AT&T and Hewlett-Packard were able to make the seemingly unlikely case to Congress that in penalizing Toshiba, it would also harm virtually the entire American electronics industry.

By the lopsided margin of 92–5, the Senate had voted in June 1987 to punish Toshiba for a national security breach by one of its subsidiaries, the Toshiba Machine Company. The subsidiary had admitted to illegally selling to the Soviet Union high-tech machines that could make Russian submarines harder to detect by the US Navy.

When the story of the illegal sales broke, congressional reaction reached an emotional pitch reminiscent of that following Pearl Harbor. In no mood to distinguish between the parent and the guilty offspring, members of the House and Senate raced to pass a bill that would ban Toshiba products from the United States for two to five years. Calling the sales "treason," a group of House members demolished a Toshiba radio with sledgehammers in front of the Capitol, and on the floor of the House others were threatening to "crucify Toshiba commercially." In the Senate, Jake Garn of Utah, a dedicated anticommunist who had been trying to tighten export controls throughout the Ford, Carter, and Reagan years, seized on the national security aspects of the scandal to pass the retaliatory Toshiba measure as an amendment to the trade bill.

The day after the vote, the chairman and president of the parent company in Tokyo resigned, accepting personal responsibility for the sales and expressing regret for the wrongdoing of a subsidiary. The resignations also signaled Toshiba's decision to fight back in

Washington. The way things were going, the company stood to lose $2.7 billion a year in business in the United States.

Toshiba was operating on several different levels in the US economy. Surprisingly, it turned out to be enmeshed from top to bottom in the nation's high-tech establishment. At that time, Toshiba was the largest supplier of essential computer chips to electronics companies in the United States. In particular, its mass-produced megabit – combining the capabilities of four 256k chips – not only allowed American manufacturers to make things smaller, but also, according to the Tokyo company's Washington lawyer-lobbyist, David P. Houlihan, gave them the opportunity to create new products with low-power utilization, such as fine-definition TV screens. And once a US company started using megabits in its output, it had a monkey on its back. More were always needed, and the principal source was Toshiba.

On still another level of its US operations, Toshiba was employing 6,000 Americans in the manufacture of laptop computers in California, microwave ovens in Tennessee, copying machines in South Dakota, and engineering controls in Oklahoma.

Of even more significance was the company's vast custom-parts operation, which made products that became essential equipment to the largest of American companies. The Japanese firm was supplying special components to Hewlett-Packard, AT&T, Compaq, and a host of other high-tech concerns. The list went on. If Toshiba products were banned from the US market, it turned out, billions of dollars in sales would be lost to such giants as IBM, Honeywell, Bell & Howell, Apple, Xerox, Motorola, and United Technologies.

According to Houlihan, no one – not even Toshiba executives – had realized how deeply and vulnerably the company had penetrated the US market. Toshiba knew, of course, who its customers were, what they were buying and how much they were spending. But when ordering special equipment, American companies usually would not tell Toshiba how it would be used or how important it was to the company. If they did so, the price might go up.

So as Congress contemplated sanctions against Toshiba, US companies began approaching members with stories of potential commercial disaster if Toshiba were to be banned from the US market.

"I just came on the market with this $700 million investment," said one CEO. "The product took me 18 months to design, and it will take me 16 months more to redesign if you knock out this Toshiba part."

The CEO of another company went to his Massachusetts senators with this problem: "My company started in 1980 and it now does $80 million worth of business a year – half of it with the Defense Department. Toshiba is vitally involved with what we do. If this ban goes through, I'd lose that 50 percent. It won't just be cut down – it will be wiped out."

This kind of reaction didn't come just from large companies. A young electronics engineer who was designing a computer for the Detroit School System for learning-disabled children phoned to say that a specially designed Toshiba product was crucial to the product he was creating. "I've spent two years designing my computer. What am I going to do now?"

Such calls had the value of pure gold to Houlihan as a lobbyist, but he and the two special legislative counsels Toshiba had hired for this case, James R. Jones, former Democratic congressman and senior member of the House Ways and Means Committee, and Leonard Garment, a well-connected Republican, were wary about how they should be handled. They decided that as registered agents of a Japanese company the worst thing they could do would be to act as a secretariat for the spontaneous grassroots eruption of American interests to save Toshiba; a coordinated effort by a Japanese company would surely backfire. The response on the Hill had to be entirely American – from Toshiba's very impressive list of blue-chip customers, and from its employees.

Accordingly, when they took the calls from American companies, Houlihan and Burt Wides, the Washington lawyer for Toshiba's American subsidiary, encouraged the callers to take their problems to Congress personally. The American side of the lobbying effort became organized when the American Electronics Association, the Computer and Business Equipment Manufacturers Association, the Computer and Communications Industries Association, and the National Association of Manufacturers stepped into the case.

At first, the lobbying of the American companies met a hailstorm of opposition. "It might hurt you," they were told by legislators, "but, by God, we've got to teach the world a lesson." The sentiment was running strongly and seemingly implacably against Toshiba.

Instead of trying to fight the tide on the Hill, Toshiba's

Washington lobbyists turned their attention to what Tokyo should be doing to make sure the security breach wouldn't happen again. Japan would have to recognize that it was facing not just another trade problem, but a national security problem for both countries – one that could only be dealt with through an independent investigation and the passage of a model export-control compliance program to which all Japanese businesses would subscribe. It was essential to show Congress and the American people that Japan was taking this matter seriously.

When there was significant movement in the Japanese Diet (parliament) on legislation, the information was shared with those running the independent American effort. Now that they could report progress in Japan, the US company lobbyists began to do better. Their basic message was, punish the guilty, but don't punish the innocent along with them. Japan, they argued, understands the seriousness of the matter and has taken steps to avoid future occurrences.

There was evidence that the case was beginning to turn around. The Toshiba lobbying team felt confident that all the leaders of the House–Senate conference that was to consider the Garn amendment in March 1988 had been convinced that the parent company didn't deserve punishment. Everything was going fine when, on the day before the conference was to be held, the *Washington Post* and *The New York Times* reported that a Japanese court passing sentence on Toshiba Machine had levied only a small fine for the crime – what Congress saw as a slap on the wrist.

Angry members of the conference put sanctions back into the trade bill: Toshiba, the parent company, would be banned from contract sales to the US government, accounting for about 5 percent of the $2.7 billion Toshiba earns here every year. At the time of writing the case was still not resolved, but a drop from $2.7 billion to $130 million a year in penalties qualifies as winning in Washington.

The bankers defeat Congress

It was a credit-union official who first recognized the tremendous scope of citizen outrage that could be unleashed if Congress meddled with savings accounts and stock dividends.

"No one knows what kind of public opinion engine we've turned on," said Bruce Jolly when the nation's financial institutions appealed to the public in an attempt to repeal an interest- and dividend-withholding act. "With the credit unions, the banks, and the savings and loans, we can reach virtually every citizen in America."

That was the beginning of the largest, best-organized grassroots campaign since the anti-Vietnam War marches – a textbook example of mobilizing grassroots support to get something done on Capitol Hill. Once started, it took on a life of its own. More than 22 million letters, postcards, Mailgrams, and telephone calls inundated Congress, telling the people's elected representatives not to permit taxes to be withheld at the source on savings accounts and dividends on securities.

Taxing interest and dividends before they reached the recipient was not really a new idea. It had been defeated over and over again since 1962, when President John F. Kennedy suggested it as a way to plug loopholes in the tax code. But in 1982, Bob Dole, chairman of the Senate Finance Committee, and Dan Rostenkowski, head of the Ways and Means Committee, introduced it once more. People were apt to forget to declare the interest on small savings deposits and dividend checks, and with the deficit rising steeply, the government could not afford to let the money trickle away. The measure didn't seem to stand much chance of passage, but Dole did not give up. He managed to persuade a majority of his committee to report the bill out. On July 22, with Congress preparing to recess, the bill squeaked through the full Senate by a 50–47 vote. Less than two weeks later, a Senate–House conference hastily approved it.

Most of the nation's financial institutions, which would have been forced to bear the multibillion-dollar cost of implementing the law, quickly closed ranks and girded for a fight. At the annual meeting of the American Bankers Association, the organization's board of directors met several times to map out a strategy. They decided to find out how banking customers felt about the new law and to undertake a public education program. In less time than it usually takes to approve a loan at the corner bank, the board had agreed to send a group of "banking advisors" around the country to tell the public what the provisions of the law would mean to savers.

Within a few days, bankers everywhere were speaking out against the law. "It is the consumer rip-off of the year," California banker

Elizabeth Kuchinski told an audience in Boise, Idaho. She hit hard on the ideas that savings were "sacrosanct," particularly for the elderly, and, as an afterthought, that the huge cost of implementing the program would be passed on to the consumer. Elsewhere, other bankers speaking in public insisted that "a consumer volcano is about to erupt."

By November the Washington headquarters of the ABA had set up four focus groups of typical savers to learn how the public felt. A focus group is an advertising and marketing research tool in which potential users of a product are brought together in an effort to determine the product's chances in the marketplace. The discussions are intended to bring out the good points, as well as the flaws, of the product in the eyes of the consumers.

The ABA's focus groups uncovered a great deal of resentment among the participants to the idea of withholding at the source. People considered the measure a new tax law that Congress had imposed in secrecy. Furthermore, they resented the implication by Congress that they were tax cheats. Those were the good points in the product from the bankers' point of view. The flaw was that the people were annoyed at the financial community, too. Why isn't my bank protecting me against such an outrage? they were asking.

With this research in hand, the bankers began asking individual customers what should be done about the law. "Repeal" was the overwhelming response, so the association promptly produced "repeal kits." Nine thousand bank members of the ABA requested these information packets, which were to be sent to the local media and to be used by bank employees who might be asked about the issue. The kit estimated the cost to savers in lost compounding and dividend reinvestment opportunities at $1.5 billion – a figure that quickly became a "magic number," quoted again and again. Another $1.5 billion was shown as the cost for financial institutions to turn themselves into tax collectors.

In Washington the lobbyists' first priority was to delay the law's effective date of January 1, 1983. ABA's officers told Congress they couldn't possibly get the necessary paperwork done by that time. New computer software would have to be developed, forms would have to be filled out by all customers and filed, thousands of bank employees would have to be trained to answer questions and deal with the people who wouldn't understand what was going on. With the concurrence of the Treasury Department, Dole agreed to give the banks a six-month reprieve.

Only a few weeks later, as the 98th Congress convened in January 1983, 23 repeal bills were introduced in the House during the first two days of the session. The four most important bills had 96 cosponsors. And the six-month delay gave the major opponents – the ABA, the US League of Savings Institutions, the Credit Union National Association, and the Gray Panthers (a senior-citizens' group) – the chance to mount a really mammoth campaign.

The members of the coalition knew their fight was sure to be expensive and bitter. For one thing, not all the banks were in the fight together. The big banks, whose computers could be more easily adapted to deduct 10 percent from the savings interest, didn't care to risk opposing the Reagan Administration, which supported the law. Representatives of several large banks visited the White House to tell the President that they were not involved in the repeal effort. For another, the repeal fight appeared virtually unwinnable, at least if history was any guide.

ABA lobbyist Fred Mutz looked into the annals of Congress and found that even though hundreds of petitions for repeal had been presented, in 200 years of congressional history only two laws actually had been repealed. Not even an inveterate gambler would have viewed those odds as playable. Since most bankers are not inveterate gamblers, the lobbyists decided to rethink the repeal effort. Dole was invited to address the bankers' leadership conference, a summit session of 450 top banking officials, to discuss a compromise. But the tone of the senator's speech appeared to make compromise impossible.

Dole threatened the banking community with higher taxes and other legislative reprisals if the repeal campaign wasn't stopped. Mutz recalled that the senator refused to answer questions from the audience after delivering his ultimatum and then held a widely reported press conference immediately afterward decrying the bankers' stand. This left the bankers without a face-saving way out. They voted to put all their resources behind repeal.

A huge direct-mail campaign was begun. Material sent to elderly savers informed them they would have to fill in complicated questionnaires in order to receive exemptions from withholding. Savings customers were told they would lose money in compound interest, because the 10 percent withheld would not be included in the compounding. Forecasts on how much the cost of services would have to be raised to make up for the cost of administering the deductions were sent out as "statement stuffers" to all customers of financial institutions. In all, 14 million flyers went out. Presumably, at least one found its way into every household that had ever been on the rolls of a bank, a savings and loan, or a credit union.

To reach those who kept their money under a mattress and didn't get any mail from banks, editorials were placed in newspapers all over the country, large and small, daily and weekly. Although the *Washington Post* and many other big-city papers sided with Dole and President Reagan (in an interview Dole dubbed the bankers "the truly greedy"), hundreds of small and medium-sized papers around the country ran a canned editorial supplied by the bankers. Titled "Savers Warning," it ended with a tagline that turned out to be extremely effective: "If you would like to tell your lawmakers how you feel about advancing the government 10 percent of the earnings from your savings and investments, write to them at [address]."

The country wrote to Washington as never before. The Senate Finance Committee had to handle 100,000 letters a month, and not just boilerplate. One saver wrote: "To apply for an exemption I have to fill out a government form with each financial institution where I have an account. Fortunately I am physically able to do so, but many of my friends are not. Does this mean that they will lose the use of 10 percent of their earnings on interest and dividends? Many retired people depend on this money for their day-to-day expenses for food, clothing, medical bills, and housing."

Senator Charles Percy (R, Ill.) received 300,000 letters on the withholding issue – 50,000 more than he had received on all legislative issues combined the year before.

In March, Senator Robert Kasten (R, Wis.) combined all congressional efforts at repeal by trying to attach a tax rider to a jobs bill. A rider is a provision that wouldn't have a chance of passing on its own merits and so is attached to an important bill – that is, it goes along for the "ride" through the legislative process. If the important bill becomes law, so does the rider. Kasten was unable to get the bill passed, but he did win agreement from the Senate leadership that the repeal would be attached to a trade bill scheduled to come up on – appropriately enough – April 15. Before the vote, the ABA again turned to research. In a national telephone survey, the bankers found that 71 percent of the people supported repeal. Not surprisingly, the ABA did not keep the results to itself. Bankers everywhere generously shared their information with all members of Congress and with the media.

Faced with this barrage, Dole retreated somewhat. He suggested that withholding be limited to convicted tax evaders, while other taxpayers would simply provide more information on their interest and dividends to the IRS. With a chance to grab the limelight, however, Senate Democrats let it be known that they were going to push for flat-out repeal, rather than a compromise.

At the last minute, with the fight almost won, the banking lobby changed its position and decided to support Dole's modified version. The banking lobbyists were eager to repair their image with the Senate Finance Committee. Dole's amendment was attached to the Caribbean Basin Initiative bill, a pet project of the President's, and it sailed through the Senate by a 91–5 vote on April 21.

But the House was not yet finished with withholding. Representative Norman E. D'Amours (D, NH) was busy collecting signatures on a discharge petition to get the repeal bill on the floor. On May 4, D'Amours had the 218 House signatures he needed. And on July 28, the Caribbean Basin Initiative swept through the House, with the repeal amendment attached, by a vote of 392–18. It subsequently passed the Senate, 91–7.

Ironically, since the law was scheduled to go into effect in July, the banks had to prepare to implement the withholding bill at the same time they were fighting to repeal it. But when it was over, they had won a historic victory: only the third outright repeal of a passed law in the last 200 years.

"We were very successful," Mutz says. "But I don't know of anyone on either side who would like to see a repeat performance. Once is enough."

The story of the savings withholding bill is a prime example of the power a concerned public can wield in Washington. In one sense, the story of the "world's biggest public opinion engine" confirms what Lynn Greenwalt, vice-president of the National Wildlife Federation, says: "When ordinary people approach their representatives and tell them what they want and get the legislation through, that's what gives lobbying its good name." However, Senator Dole and other members of the Senate Finance Committee felt that the banking interests had presented a distorted picture of the proposed legislation to the public. They believed that if it had not been called a "new tax," but simply the plugging of a draining loophole in the public treasury, it would not have aroused the ire of the 99 percent of the public who fill in their tax returns honestly.

The millions of men and women who made their legislators retreat on the savings-interest withholding measure were rich and poor, black and white, old and young. All they had in common was savings accounts – obviously a powerful stimulus to democratic action.

Saving the Day with Employees and Suppliers

How Chrysler got its loan guarantee

In 1979, when the Chrysler Corporation sought a $1.5 billion loan guarantee from the federal government, the company was a terrible credit risk. Just the year before, it had posted a loss of $2 billion, the worst earnings record in American corporate history. Still, Chrysler managed to save itself and set a lobbying precedent for American business. The company won its case for congressional support by mobilizing people in every state who would stand to lose part of their livelihood if the corporation failed.

When Chrysler headed for the Capitol to make its case, President Lee Iacocca was several notches below the legendary figure he is today, though he was even then a formidable automobile executive. Turned away by the banks, Chrysler had practically no allies when it appeared hat in hand on the doorstep of Congress to ask for a bailout.

Iacocca couldn't even count on the support of nonautomotive big business. As a public policy issue, the loan guarantee was a certified loser that deserved to lose, according to the spokesmen for the corporate boardrooms. The National Association of Manufacturers, the Business Roundtable (the public policy summit group of the CEOs of the country's biggest corporations), and the *Wall Street Journal* all opposed it. As the *Journal* put it, the American way included the freedom to fail as well as the freedom to succeed. Caught in the Red Sea of its account books, with the enemy closing in fast, the only option left for Chrysler was to produce a miracle.

In such an apparently hopeless situation, Iacocca decided to attack. His lieutenants mobilized the most varied and focused grassroots campaign the Hill had encountered in years. Iacocca was betting every Chrysler product yet to come on the theory that no economist, editorialist, or advocate of the freedom-to-fail theory could derail the loan guarantee if enough voters were for it. The case was dramatized in terms of what the company's failure would mean in economic impact on each of the 50 states.

The problem with the strategy was that Chrysler did not have plants in all 50 states. Though it was the 10th largest corporation in the country, it had major facilities in only eight states: Michigan, Missouri, Indiana, Illinois, Alabama, New York, Ohio, and Delaware. And those 16 votes would not come close to swinging the Senate.

Nevertheless, a miracle was produced. Through imaginative networking, the company was able to prove that it was intimately tied to the economy of every state in the union. The pitch wasn't too different from the song about the knee bone being connected to the thigh bone.

As a grassroots nucleus, Chrysler had 4,000 dealerships spread through every state and congressional district, each of which provided jobs for local residents. And then it had very important suppliers, all of them employing or supporting a significant number of voters. Chrysler was the second-largest purchaser of glass in the country and the third-largest user of tires and radios. Its sun visors were made in one part of the United States, its carpets in another – and those visors and carpets were packaged in boxes that were made somewhere else. Moreover, the nails for the shipping crates that carried all these parts were made in yet another state. Even the suppliers of coffee, candy, and soft-drink machines in the factories and dealer showrooms were mobilized.

Soon, the potential failure of Chrysler seemed to involve an economic collapse of a large number of companies, rather than just lost jobs for a few thousand auto workers. Chrysler's chief lobbyists, Tommy Boggs on the Democratic side and Tom Korologos on the Republican, could document that 600,000 jobs from coast to coast and from the Great Lakes to the Gulf were directly tied to the company's continued viability. Combining all these elements,

Chrysler carefully staged a national campaign that never lost its local flavor. The company had an army ready and willing to march.

This army wasn't going to march only to Washington. It was figuratively marching to every editor, to every TV anchor, to every radio commentator in every state. The public had to be persuaded through the media that they had a stake in saving Chrysler Corporation.

On days when key votes were scheduled, the Chrysler army swarmed over Capitol Hill, and blue knit hats with the company's familiar logo were visible everywhere. Meanwhile, support groups proliferated. The National Association for the Advancement of Colored People traced 1 percent of black America's income to Chrysler-related employment and made its voice heard. So did the US Conference of Mayors, whose urban economics policy committee was chaired by Detroit mayor Coleman Young. Even the competition got into the spirit of the campaign. One Chevrolet–Honda dealer wrote an open letter to his customers: "If we can't sell you a Chevrolet or a Honda, buy a Chrysler."

The United Auto Workers added its considerable strength as an equal partner with Chrysler in the lobbying effort. The UAW had chits to collect all over the Capitol for previous election support, and its clout reached inside the Carter White House. The time had come for demanding repayment on an enormous stack of IOUs held by the union.

The Michigan congressional delegation was particularly creative in drumming up support from colleagues in other states. Except for Representative David Stockman, every member from Michigan favored the loan guarantee. Their efforts were unrelenting.

Representative William Brodhead met with the Detroit City Council and urged its members to ask their fellow councilmen in other cities to speak up for Chrysler to their own members of Congress. Brodhead also asked the New York congressional delegation for a quid pro quo. He reminded these colleagues that a few years earlier he had supported the New York City financial bailout at a time when President Gerald Ford was quoted in a New York *Daily News* headline as telling the city to "Drop Dead." The broad-based effort also meant Chrysler could tailor arguments to every member of Congress, no matter what his or her ideological bent. To liberals, the lobbyists stressed the social issues – primarily, the possibility that

Chrysler's bankruptcy alone could increase the national unemployment rate by 1 percent. To conservatives, the lobbyists played upon the company's role in national defense. It was unthinkable, they argued, that the free world's largest maker of tanks should be allowed to go bust, no matter how much money it lost.

The vote in the Senate was close, but the bailout passed, 53–44. The House followed suit. Two years later, Chrysler ceremoniously repaid the loan, taking the government off the hook and giving the US Treasury a tidy profit on stock options. And the lobbying effort had left a useful phrase in the congressional lexicon. To this day, when a member of Congress is dead serious about the importance of a vote solicited from a colleague, the member will insist: "This is my Chrysler!"

The Chrysler bailout was a larger-than-life effort. In the end, it had everything going for it: widespread grassroots support, bipartisan congressional teamwork, skilled lobbying, and in-depth media exposure.

Creating a groundswell without a real constituency

It wasn't difficult to identify the potential constituency that would support Chrysler and oppose credit-card surcharges, nuclear proliferation, and taxes on Betamaxes, but how would you go about creating a groundswell for an issue that has no popular appeal and no defined group with any logical reason to espouse it? Simple – you go to one of the most remarkable computers in America, programmed to a social scientist's dream.

It was the invention of Jonathan Robbin, who changed the world of grassroots communication when he fed 6 billion bytes of raw population data from the US Census into a computer. Robbin pressed some buttons and concluded that the entire United States consists of only 12 social groups living in 40 types of neighborhood, which are the same anywhere in the country. These neighborhoods, which he called clusters, have been given pop designations, such as Blue Blood Estates and Downtown Dixie Style. The people who live in them can be expected to react similarly on social and economic issues whether they live in Bangor or San Diego.

"You can go to sleep in Fairfield, Connecticut, and wake up in

Pasadena," Robbin declares, "but except for the palm trees you're really in the same place."

With this insight, he founded a company called Claritas in Alexandria, Va., which very successfully helps marketers sell anything from shaving cream to dune buggies. In the hands of knowledgeable political consultants, the cluster data are becoming a prime source of national constituencies for virtually any legislative purpose. Utilities used the clusters to find voters who favored deregulation of natural gas. A communications company, by going to the clusters and picking the right groups, located enough people in selected states to show a doubting Senate, through letters, calls, and even personal visits, that a considerable number of Americans favored an access charge for their telephones.

Approached on an issue from their own point of view, people will write letters, go door-to-door, hold meetings, and solicit other workers. They like to be asked, and they get their backs into the campaigns with as much enthusiasm as if they were working for a charismatic candidate.

Claritas has broadened the definition of an affinity group. Whereas such a group was once invariably founded on common professional or ethnic interests, it now includes masses of people linked by lifestyle and philosophy. In practice, good politicians, demagogues, and successful lobbyists have mined that lode for hundreds of years. The genius of Jonathan Robbin was that he put it on a computer.

6

Winning with Established Grassroots Organizations

Most of the groups we have been dealing with up to this point have been ad hoc associations organized for one specific purpose – the bank customers, the video stores, Toshiba's customers. Such groups are unlikely to stay together for longer than it takes to write the required letter to a congressman, appear at the Capitol, and read the thank-you notes after the cause has been won.

Some grassroots groups, however, have been organized for years, getting new recruits and winning their legislative battles with greater frequency than the laws of probability would predict. The National Wildlife Federation, for instance, keeps a close vigil on the Interior Department's handling of mineral, grazing, and logging rights, and alerts members to any threat to trout streams, wilderness areas, and wildlife habitats. When any of these are endangered, the federation sends in its "big guns" – constituents who can explain the problem to their senators and representatives. Virtually the same techniques are utilized in different areas by the senior-citizen and gun lobbies.

If you have an issue that one of these groups or hundreds of others can rally around, your chance of winning will automatically improve. Always remember, however, that these groups are very specialized; they look at each issue from a narrow point of view, and if it is important enough to them, you may have to compromise in order to attach your issue to theirs. One of the most powerful of these groups is the American Association of Retired People (AARP), which focuses on everything that affects people over 50. AARP members are the most faithful lobbyists that anyone pushing an issue could ask for.

The AARP in Action

At the end of a long session on the budget in the summer of 1985, Senators Fritz Hollings and Pete Domenici were comparing notes on the pressures they had been subjected to on one piece of legislation, a plan to cut the cost-of-living increases on Social Security payments.

"I've had more mail on that than on anything I can remember since I've been in the Senate," said Domenici, a New Mexico Republican who was then chairman of the Senate Budget Committee.

"So have I," replied Hollings, a South Carolina Democrat. "But have you ever gotten anything like this?" He reached into his pocket and fished out a clipping from a newsletter put out by the American Association of Retired Persons. At the top of the clipping, a story about the Social Security issue from the perspective of recipients, was a handwritten note: "Please read this!" And it was signed, simply, "Mother."

Mrs Hollings isn't the only senatorial mother on the AARP membership roster. Plenty of congressional parents have plunked down the $5 membership fee to win all kinds of discount benefits on prescriptions, travel, and insurance, plus enviable political potency.

With 20 million members, the AARP gains victories through the sheer weight of numbers. It overwhelms the entire Congress, rather than focusing on specific legislators or concentrating on a specific political party. The membership is so large, in fact, that it cuts across every social and political division.

The one thing all these people have in common is that the AARP found and recruited them by direct mail, with the lure of special discounts and demonstrated Washington muscle. Not all of them are retired. In fact, the eligibility age has been going down like a limbo bar as the years go by, adding the vitality of a large middle-aged contingent to an organization that was full of bounce to begin with.

In order to win on the big issues – Social Security, Medicare, Supplemental Security Income (SSI) – the AARP comes into battle with finely honed weapons. It has an in-house research department for scientific polling, which operates almost continuously on all kinds of issues.

Don't make the mistake of calling the AARP a "public interest" group, however. "We have a very well-defined constituency," says

Marty Corry, one of the organization's legislative specialists. "It happens to be a large one, but it is still defined by age and by the concerns that all people over a certain age have in common."

The AARP's very size leads to some surprises. Apart from its newsletter and its slick magazine, *Modern Maturity*, which pleasantly offers general-interest articles and issue briefings, the AARP rarely does full mailings to its members. Because its membership is so diverse, the organization went on for years believing that a political action committee would be impossible to form. Yet almost as soon as it was organized in the last few years, the AARP's PAC became one of the largest and, predictably, most effective of all such committees. The variety of political opinion within AARP is no barrier to the selection of issues the organization is willing to go to bat for. The only test is an issue's effect on the fortunes of the aging.

AARP members are so responsive that huge mailings aren't necessary. "We get more letters from your members than from anyone else," congressional staffers tell Corry, who is not surprised.

"We know that our members participate in the process," he says. "That's our winning margin. If our members are upset, they sit down and write letters to Congress, state legislatures, and city councils."

Because of their organization's grassroots power, the 30 volunteers from the AARP's National Legislative Council who come to Washington each fall for their annual legislative meeting are treated by public officials like Neiman-Marcus buyers at a fashion show. The leaders of the House and the Senate, the chairmen of the key committees, and representatives of the White House and the Department of Health and Human Services come to present their programs for the next year and get feedback.

When it comes time to compromise on Capitol Hill, AARP's widespread membership again comes into play. Unlike Washington players with a narrower agenda, the organization operates with considerable give-and-take.

"Because our members span all political affiliations and brackets, we have to address a whole package of legislation," says Corry. "Suppose a package includes some hard-to-swallow items – say, A, B, and C. If items D through R are acceptable, and items S through Z are first-rate, we'll make a decision to back every letter of the alphabet so that the good doesn't get lost with the bad. That is the main difference between lobbying for AARP and lobbying for a corporation or industry association. They have the luxury of concentrating on one small issue. We're always looking at the big picture."

Single-Issue Voters

The "single-issue voter" has been on the American political scene from the Vermont Green Mountain Boys and the Whisky Rebellion onward. Among the first to show muscle as voters rather than revolutionaries were the farmers, through the National Grange, and the gun interests and enthusiasts, through the National Rifle Association. What the founders of the Conservative Caucus and Common Cause added, though, was the use of the electronic revolution to forge national unions of people who believe vehemently in a tenet that perhaps 2 percent of their fellow citizens would fight for.

In the precomputer grassroots days of the early 1960s, a voter might make a forceful case at the Kiwanis or American Legion meeting against voting for a specific candidate because of views on abortion, defense spending, or school prayer. But chances were slim that these ideas would translate into a large volume of letters to Congress. The single-issue voter in Butte, Montana, felt like a voice shouting in the wilderness; he had no idea he had a soul brother in Brownsville, Texas – or even in his own neighborhood.

What the issue-oriented direct-mail producers have done is take that voice in the wilderness and turn it into a roar. Today the one-issue voter has a direct-mail link and an organization that is happy to accept his contributions when he is ready to put his money where his mouth is. The computers have formed a network, and normally independent officeholders can get fatally enmeshed in it. Two percent of the population in almost any state can swing a tight election.

Many single-issue voters are not content to limit their participation in the legislative process to writing, telephoning, or visiting their congressional representatives. They believe in showing up in force in Washington to demonstrate their strength. They come by the thousands – by plane, by rail, by bus, by car, and, on one never-to-be-forgotten day in 1978, by tractors that paralyzed Washington traffic until noon.

The tractor drivers were angry farmers from the American Agricultural Movement, who started their grassroots roll-in from Colorado to protest low farm prices and picked up recruits with more heavy equipment in states along the way. The amount of armor they had amassed as they reached the District line would have impressed Rommel. Their plan to dramatize the economic depression in farm country had only one flaw: like everyone else in Washington, the members of Congress the farmers wanted to lobby were kept fuming on the roads leading into the city. Their case was not helped by the traffic jam or the damage to the grass on the Mall. (There was a more pleasant postscript in 1979, when the men and women of the AAM came back to Washington, once more with the heavy stuff, right in the middle of a snowstorm. They were able to pitch in by digging out cars and cleaning streets.)

If you have a cause that can become an emotional issue for a number of people anywhere in the United States, the cheapest, most effective way of forcing the government to deal with the issue is to organize a march on Washington. Marches are so much a part of mass lobbying that the Metropolitan Police Department of the District of Columbia will tell you the rules of approved conduct for protests and the United States Park Police will provide you with a map showing the best locations to stage the protest. Only in America!

Much of this mass protest is centered in Lafayette Park, across the street from 1600 Pennsylvania Avenue, where the President could, if so inclined, look out the window at some 1,400 demonstrations a year representing every imaginable point of view.

Each year on January 22, the anniversary of the Supreme Court's landmark abortion decision, *Roe* v. *Wade*, about 50,000 men and women parade down Pennsylvania Avenue to the Supreme Court and the Capitol to protest that decision. The coalition that defends a woman's right to choose whether to terminate her pregnancy often makes the same trek. None of these people come to Washington because they like to march. They come because they want the country to see them marching on the six o'clock news and on the front page of the morning paper – an important part of the lobbying process. They're sending a message up to the Hill and back down to the grassroots.

After the march the paraders fan out on Capitol Hill to lobby the senators and representatives they sent to Washington. Regardless of how the elected official votes on the issue, the constituent will be welcomed in the office. Formal appointment or not, no congressman will deliberately insult a voter with enough interest to come to Washington to see him.

Even people who do not have the right to petition their own government use the Washington stage to petition ours. Before the Iranian revolution, masked supporters of the Ayatollah Khomeini marched past our offices on H Street every day at the noon hour, denouncing the Shah. A few months later, when Khomeini's government was in place, the Shah's supporters were walking the same route. The only people who didn't change were the network crews who beamed the marches around the world on TV. Foreigners have learned, along with Americans, that when you tell your story in Washington, you're telling it back home with special emphasis.

It isn't just the liberal senators and representatives who get forceful messages from single-issue voters. Senator Jake Garn, who holds a perfect set of conservative credentials, gets exercised about single-issue lobbyists who pepper him with threats.

"They come in and say, 'If you're not for me on this issue, we're going to do everything possible to get rid of you'," Garn says. "That doesn't play very well with me. I say, 'Look, I cast thousands of votes around here, so I don't care what the persuasion is – whether it is abortion, school prayer, sale of arms to Jordan – just to organize a group for the purpose of defeating one issue without caring about anything else is a dangerous precedent!'"

Bill Hamilton, Washington lobbyist for the Planned Parenthood Federation of America, a prominent target of single-issue voters, takes it philosophically: "In opinion poll after opinion poll, the people of the US say that they prefer a woman's right to choice. Congressional candidates can read and understand opinion polls as well as or better than most people. They believe us, they like us. But they fear the antiabortionists. It's tough fighting a bloc vote."

When the Conservative Caucus points out that 13 senators were not reelected after voting for the Panama Canal treaty, the group doesn't claim that this issue alone brought them down. Similarly, the

American Israel Political Action Committee (AIPAC), the Israel lobby in Washington, does not claim that Charles Percy lost his senatorial reelection campaign in Illinois just because he voted to sell AWACs to Saudi Arabia.

But the implication that single-issue voters can skew election results permeates the atmosphere on the Hill. Some senators and congressmen who have chosen not to run for reelection have said the pressure of united true believers like these is just too much to withstand. Like smart prize-fighters who don't want to become punch-drunk, they decide to retire undefeated.

Most single-issue organizations have a relatively short vogue, and a secure legislator usually can wait them out. The gun lobby, however, has been taking aim for 115 years on representatives and senators who consider guns somewhat on a par with rattlesnakes and cyanide.

The National Rifle Association

With 3 million members, the National Rifle Association is smaller than many other organizations that try to have an impact on legislation, but it carries just as much, or more, clout.

NRA has never deviated from its narrow reading of the Second Amendment to the Constitution, which forbids infringement upon the people's right to keep and bear arms. The NRA is at once the granddaddy of grassroots lobbying groups, a pioneer in modern direct-mail techniques, and the prototype for the single-issue organizations that sprung up in the 1970s.

The NRA stalks legislation the way some of its members hunt game – with patience and a good aim. When Peter Rodino, former chairman of the House Judiciary Committee and a strong gun-control advocate, kicked the carcass of a newly passed Senate gun bill and pronounced it "dead on arrival," NRA lobbyist James Jay Baker said he didn't mind waiting for the resurrection.

Many editorial writers have condemned the NRA as an insensitive organization advocating the indiscriminate sale of guns and ammunition regardless of the mental and moral standing of the purchaser, but the association maintains it is only defending the Constitution. Charges that unrestricted handgun ownership begets a higher murder rate are answered with the slogan, "Guns don't kill; people do," proclaimed from millions of bumper stickers.

The rifle association has been the role model for modern grassroots lobbying. Generations of legislators have felt the effectiveness of a barrage of calls and visits by aroused hunters and gun-shop owners objecting to any sign of movement along the "slippery slope to gun control." NRA's methods of being heard in Congress were well-developed at a time when most other single-issue organizations were still naïve about their potential for political action. Its techniques have been studied and copied during the last 35 years by business, labor, and professional societies looking for more clout on the Hill.

The NRA membership is always ready at the snap of a computer key to swamp Congress, a state legislature, or a city council with angry protests. This grassroots penmanship is backed with awesome voting power – a bloc vote of 3–4 percent that can readily swing a close election. NRA's belt is notched over and over to celebrate the fall of a long roster of politicians who didn't believe or didn't care that "if guns are outlawed, only outlaws will have guns."

Despite polls that consistently have shown that most of the American public supports gun control, no restrictive legislation has cleared Congress since the fairly ineffective Gun Control Act of 1968, which was passed in response to the public outcry after the assassinations of Martin Luther King and Robert Kennedy.

Until his retirement at the end of 1988, Peter Rodino was an implacable foe of the National Rifle Association. In 1980 he teamed up with Ted Kennedy in an attempt to put something more than a bark into the 1968 act – a bill that mandated throwing owners of unlicensed handguns into jail for a year. The NRA promptly brought the news to the hustings, and a legislative posse was organized to go after Kennedy and Rodino. Sportsmen were told that the bill's sponsors were opposed to hunting rifles, long guns, and sporting pistols, in addition to handguns – a charge the legislators kept denying up to the day the bill was shelved.

Not even the assassination attempt on President Reagan on March 30, 1981 brought enthusiasm in Congress for a stronger gun-control law, at least in part because the President, a lifelong NRA member, made it clear that he remained opposed to any sort of gun-control legislation. Rodino could not generate winning impetus either from the startling murders of John Lennon and Dr Michael Halberstam, the prominent Washington physician and writer who was shot by an intruder in his home.

There have been other signs that public perception of handgun ownership is changing. Many liberal Americans don't like the idea of being armed but believe that gun ownership is necessary to protect home and family against urban crime. Carl Rowan, the liberal Washington columnist who has waged a fight against NRA for years, became a *cause célèbrè* for the association when he shot and slightly wounded an intruder at 2.00 AM in his backyard. NRA, which is very skilled at presenting its issues on the Hill, couldn't have asked for a better publicity break.

This changing mood in the country is confirmed by Roger Craver, the leading direct-mail fund-raiser for liberal causes and an accurate forecaster of which issues will make people on his mailing lists dig into their pockets: "We can't get our people excited about gun control. They are concerned about safety and they want to be able to buy guns to protect themselves."

NRA's strong position on the Hill leaves James Jay Baker with comfortable options on how he chooses to use his lobbying time. "We never try to persuade senators and representatives who have consistently voted against us in the past," he says. "We are not going to change their minds. Likewise, we don't waste the association's money on mail from the districts to the legislators we know are for us."

Senator James McClure of Idaho, the leading opponent of gun control in the Senate, wryly disagrees with totally ignoring the proven opposition. "You don't go after the already damned," he told us, "but once in a while you can save a soul." McClure is so completely identified as an enthusiastic NRA supporter that his colleagues, rushing onto the floor to vote on a gun issue they haven't been briefed on, can and do base their aye or nay entirely on how he intends to vote.

Baker and his associates focus their efforts on wooing the sometimes-I'm-for-you, sometimes-I'm-against-you vote. Plying this softer area, they have found, helps strengthen the pro-gun constituency. Baker's technique is effective: "If one of these wavering members is uncertain about the feelings in his home district about the issue or its economic impact, we fly in one or two people from the district – usually people who own gun shops – to talk to him."

While he does not lobby the already-convinced, Baker hardly ignores them either. He drops in for a chat and stays in touch with both the members and their staffs. Besides making social calls, he is always on hand to help reelection campaigns. The NRA's political action committee – started in 1977 when the association decided to augment its model grassroots system with hands-on, face-to-face lobbying – distributed $4.8 million raised from its members to state and federal candidates in 1985–6. Of this sum, $909,000 was spent on behalf of senators and representatives who had voted with NRA position on the interstate sale of handguns.

The NRA is sensitive to charges that it has no agenda other than defeating gun-control laws. It points with pride to a number of public-service programs with national outreach. Lobbying, Baker says, takes up only 20 percent of the association's budget and only one floor of its eight-story building in the heart of downtown Washington. Among its activities are teaching the responsible use of firearms to the Boy Scouts, instructing police departments across the country in gun safety, and training the US Olympic Shooting Team.

As effective as it has been, the NRA, like all other lobbies, doesn't always come out on top. In late 1981, its persistent attack on the Bureau of Alcohol, Tobacco, and Firearms, the Treasury Department agency charged with enforcing the 1968 Gun Control Act, suddenly achieved the wrong goal. To demonstrate the "entire shabby history of the bureau and the Gun Control Act," the association produced a half-hour film for TV called *It Can't Happen Here*. In the film, Representative John Dingell, one of the leaders of the House and an ardent hunter, called the BATF a "jack-booted group of fascists who are a shame and a disgrace to our country." The Gun Owners of America went so far as to accuse the Bureau of using Nazi tactics.

The Reagan administration reacted to the concerted campaign by deciding to turn over enforcement of the Act to the Secret Service. This was not what NRA wanted at all. It had hoped merely to weaken BATF, laying the groundwork for repeal of the Gun Control Act. Under the jurisdiction of the Secret Service, enforcement promised to be even more efficient.

The NRA thus was forced to do a flip-flop on the issue. It began to fight to preserve its long-time enemy BATF – a turnaround that enraged some of the gun lobby's staunchest supporters in Congress and the administration.

Although, like ordinary lobbyists, the NRA can sometimes meet itself coming and going, it is able to fend for itself on any issue involving guns. And when it ventures beyond its single issue to take a stand on other matters, such as protecting the sanctity of the wilderness, it enters into coalitions with other national organizations, including the National Wildlife Federation, the Izaak Walton League, and Ducks Unlimited.

James Jay Baker says about bills pertaining to guns: "Each time an allegation is made we will have to answer with the facts. The facts are on our side." He continues, "We're going to give the members everything they request to make the bill understandable."

"And," he adds, invoking the heart and soul of his organization's continuing and growing strength, "we're going to send three million letters to our members asking them to help us. That will generate one million communications to Congress."

Israel Grows American Grassroots

When the Japanese were preparing to make a stand against protectionism in Washington several years ago, the role model the Japanese Ministry of International Trade and Industry chose to study was the Israel lobby. The question MITI wanted answered was how Israel, through the efforts of the American Israel Public Affairs Committee (AIPAC), was able to muster such strong congressional support no matter what the issue – security and arms, peace and war, trade and aid.

Thomas A. Dine, the executive director of AIPAC, laughs at the idea of being copied. He doesn't for a minute deny his lobby's success but he knows that – unlikely as it may seem – it is grassroots support that helps him do his job.

"When I go into a congressional office, the legislator and the staff know that I'm just Tom Dine, someone they know, someone they have seen around for almost 20 years," says Dine, who served his apprenticeship in foreign affairs as legislative assistant to Frank Church, a former chairman of the Senate Foreign Relations Committee.

"But they also know that I'm not coming in alone. I've got a whole army behind me. Not just American Jews. That would be only 3 percent of the population and it wouldn't make a dent in the voting of, say, Nevada or Arizona or Kansas. But in every national poll, at least 80 percent of the people questioned are for the Israelis as opposed the Arabs." And that 80 percent reaches like a rainbow from the left to the far right in Congress, arcing from Ted Kennedy to Jesse Helms.

Grassroots interest in foreign affairs is generally hard to induce in the United States. Israel is one exception; the others are NATO and Japan. "These constituencies are different," says Dine. "NATO draws on the anti-Soviet and foreign-policy establishment. Japan is supported by exporters, importers, and anticommunist groups. But Israel's support base depends on people who believe that the US has a moral commitment to the country; that Israel is a functioning democracy in a sea of absolute monarchies, theocratic dictatorships, and just plain dictatorships; and that Israel is of strategic value to the US. Most of the population of the US falls into one of those categories."

Even during the uprisings on the West Bank in 1988, this basic attitude toward Israel did not change. "As an ally of the United States, Israel is of inestimable value," says one of the spokesmen for AIPAC. "But we deal with questions deeper than political and global questions. We deal with people and their feelings. They are so important to us that we plumb their attitudes constantly.

"Some of the questionnaires we've sent out in the past four months have questions we've never asked before, such as: Do you think that Israel is using excessive force in quelling the uprisings on the West Bank? Do you think that Israel should use firearms against the demonstrators?"

These questions are aimed at gauging the backlash that the daily dose of violence in Israel might engender in the minds of the American voters. For the first time in its history, AIPAC has detected a definite upsurge in disapproval of the methods Israel has been using. "But," points out the spokesman, "we are not running for a popularity contest. Israel is fighting for its life, and the great mass of its supporters is fully aware of the life-and-death issue. The basic questions that have been asked for four years now, 'Do you trust Israel more than – less than – equally with the Arab states in the region? Do you consider Israel an ally of the United States?' are answered solidly in favor of Israel."

AIPAC knows that the votes in Congress are not going to shift measurably as long as there is solid evidence that public sentiment still favors Israel. The lobbyists from AIPAC hear almost the same sentiments from the lawmakers that they hear from the constituents.

"It's like a marriage going through a rough time," says a friend of the committee's. "There are some disagreements, and at times they look really formidable. But basically both parties are committed to keeping the union alive."

AIPAC carefully nurtures coalitions with groups that seemingly have only tangential connections with the government of Israel. Independent domestic oil-and-gas producers work with AIPAC toward a shared goal of reducing US dependence on oil imports from Arab countries. Another, more surprising, partner is the evangelical Christian movement, which supports Israel at least partially because of a literal interpretation of the Scriptures. The Bible predicts that the Messiah's arrival will be preceded by the rebirth of Israel and the rebuilding of the Temple. Fundamentalists have lobbied hard on Israel's side since the country was born in 1948.

Not that the committee must depend on partners to get its points across. A large lobbying organization for a country as small as Israel, AIPAC has 51,000 members, a $5 million annual budget, and 83 employees in Washington and other parts of the country.

Dine is responsible to a 150-member executive committee, which includes the presidents of 38 major Jewish organizations, among them the American Jewish Committee, Hadassah, and B'nai Brith. The remainder of the executive committee comprises individual political activists and leaders in local Jewish communities across the country.

The executive committee sets policy, which is carried out by five hands-on lobbyists who work the House and Senate offices. In fact, they work very hard at it. When the year-long fight over the arms sale to Jordan was at its height in Congress, in late October 1985, Dine said wearily, "Last week I saw more of Senator Dole than I saw of my wife. And I'm married, not divorced."

The $2 billion Jordan arms package recommended by the Reagan administration was considered dangerous to the Middle East peace effort by Israel – and, therefore, by AIPAC. The executive committee took a firm stance: unless serious peace talks with Israel were part of the arms deal, AIPAC would lobby against the proposal. The committee argued that providing sophisticated weapons to King Hussein of Jordan would remove his incentive to enter into peace negotiations, as well as increase the threat of an Arab offensive along the Israel–Jordan border without protecting Jordan against terrorism, its most serious security threat.

The briefing book AIPAC provided to all 535 members of Congress weighed in at slightly over three-quarters of a pound. It contained everything ever said about the Jordanian approach to peace with Israel, and it listed the weapons Hussein was shopping for – aircraft, shoulder-launched Stinger antiaircraft missiles, improved Hawk surface-to-air missiles, M-3 Bradley armored fighting vehicles, and AIM-9P Sidewinder air-to-air missiles.

The book also contained a "Dear Colleague" letter from six senators, and another from 12 members of the House. "Dear Colleagues" are missives used when one member of Congress lobbies another. Representative Charles Rangel (D, NY) says that he has received as many as 15 "Dear Colleague" letters a day. Congressmen scan them all, but reserve thorough reading and further consideration for those that can be identified as addressing constituent issues or as coming from a highly respected sender or a good friend. The letter in the AIPAC briefing-book presented chapter and verse on Jordan's air defenses, along with maps pinpointing the major air bases in Israel, Jordan, and Syria. Last but not least, it reprinted a bipartisan Senate resolution introduced by Senators John Heinz (R, Pa.) and Ted Kennedy, stating that it was the sense of the Senate that the United States should not sell advanced fighter aircraft or other arms to Jordan while King Hussein continued to oppose the Camp David peace process.

In passing, the letter also alluded to the shopping trips King Hussein had made to the USSR, France, and Britain to upgrade his arsenal, and reminded the senators and congressmen that although the administration had called Jordan a "bulwark of stability and moderation in the Middle East," the country had attacked Israel three times in 37 years and had refused to negotiate with the Israelis.

All in all, it was a perfect example of what Dine says is most important in AIPAC's lobbying efforts. "We must be trustworthy. Our information has to be accurate, it has to be timely, and it has to be relevant to policymakers. Dissertations don't get read. We must find things that are useful when someone has to vote on legislation that may mean life or death to millions of people."

In the last days of the lobbying campaign, Dine had to come up with grassroots support in a big way. "We brought citizen lobbyists in to see Congress," he recalls. "We saw 99 senators and the staff of the 100th. Senator Stennis (D, Miss,) was just too tired, but his staff said that he was against the sale. The winning solution was worked out between the majority leader, Senator Dole; the chairman of the foreign relations committee, Senator Richard Lugar (R, Ind.); and me. It was a face-saving resolution. It didn't say there wouldn't be an arms sale – which meant that President Reagan had not been thwarted. It said only that the arms sale was being put off until spring, when it was to be reconsidered if some meaningful Middle East peace talks were under way. In other words, the weapon sale was the carrot for the peace talks."

At the end of October, the Senate voted 97–1 to link the sale to "meaningful" peace overtures. It was a victory to be savored, especially since the last time Congress had debated an arms sale to a Middle Eastern country – the AWACS radar planes for Saudi Arabia – AIPAC lost by four votes on the Senate floor. In February 1986, the administration quietly withdrew its Jordan arms package, because there had been no movement on the talks.

Dine says a grassroots connection turned the 1981 AWACS loss into the 1985 Jordan win. "There were two buzzwords on the Senate floor last week," he said right after the victory. "One was Jepson and the other was Percy. Roger Jepson, the Iowa Republican who lost his reelection bid in 1984, had indicated he was going to vote against the sale of arms to Saudi Arabia and then changed his mind. Charles Percy, the Illinois Republican who headed the Senate Foreign Relations Committee and championed the AWACS deal, found that when the votes were counted in 1984 his usual urban base had eroded. The pro-Israel community actively worked against him and the public elected a new senator from Illinois."

7

Developing an Inside Strategy

Govn' Represent.

most lawmakers

Every Congress responds to three basic underpinnings of good lobbying: a logical case, a unified lobby, and a willingness to compromise. These are the key elements in a winning inside strategy.

Presenting a Logical Case

A clear and logical presentation of what a bill will and will not do, and whom it helps and whom it hurts, is essential when you present your ideas on the Hill. *to the sam't*

Not even the most accomplished writer can complete such an important text with one draft composed in the heat of the moment, so take your time. For inspiration during those long hours when draft after draft is being overhauled, keep in mind that even the framers of the Constitution labored long and hard to make their words memorable. When the constitutional debate in Philadelphia was finished and a draft written, a Committee of Style was appointed to clean up, polish, and package the document in order to sell it to "We, the people."

Check your facts, then check them again. Find precedents and supply documentation. Remember that you're writing for an audience of lawyers, who make up at least half of the Congress. Dig out the legislative history of similar cases. Order surveys and public opinion polls to back up your theories; because Congress is a representative body, these may be the most important parts of your

Be precise a accurate when presenting to sam t

presentation. If the people want what you are suggesting, you've got a case for Congress.

In 1985, lobbyist Tom Franks commissioned an extensive survey just for the 36 members of the House Ways and Means Committee in an effort to protect the tax deduction for interest on mortgages for second homes. Franks, the Washington representative of the American Land Development Association, the builders and developers of homes in vacation communities, used the survey to prove his point – that most second homes were not owned by the rich and famous, but by ordinary working couples. Up to that point, the dropping of the deduction looked like a good idea to President Reagan, Ways and Means Chairman Dan Rostenkowski, and a majority of the committee. They all thought that second homes were purely a luxury and that limitation of a tax deduction on them would not cause hardship to the owners.

"We proved that it wasn't a fat-cat issue," Franks recalls, "and we used scientific and analytic methods to do it. We were able to show Congress that most of these vacation homes are owned by Middle America, and that if you cut it off you'll hurt a lot of economies in virtually every state."

Pollsters hired by the association to survey the population that owned second homes discovered that only 50 percent did so for investment purposes. They also interviewed 5,000 vacation home owners in Coeur d'Alene, Idaho, and in Hilton Head, South Carolina, getting detailed information about their jobs, their economic standing, and the mortgage interest rates they paid. An economic-impact study projected that the government would lose $1 billion a year if the measure were enacted. A case was made that if the interest couldn't be deducted, the couples wouldn't buy the homes. Consequently, communities would lose the building revenue and construction jobs, and there would be a considerable loss of taxes at federal, state, and local levels.

Franks put the data to use by organizing "a fairly narrow coalition – just the realtors, home builders, and mayors of the cities in which second homes are an important part of the tax base." Then he wrote letters to 10,000 vacation-home owners, alerting them to the problem and telling them how to reach their representatives.

Representative Fortney Stark (D, Cal.), one of the proponents of the change, was impressed by the results. "When you get every realtor in your district writing you, and when you get all the building trades organized side-by-side with the general contractors and all of the people selling real-estate tax shelters, you have not just one small group, but 10 or 15 groups who put the fear of God into a lot of members of Congress."

Franks feels that the high cost of surveying was more than justified. "To come up to the Hill and argue a case effectively," he argues, "we needed to have the ammunition and the truth and the facts of the situation."

It is essential to master all phases of the material, because you do not want to risk a member or staffer becoming your supporter on the basis of just part of the story. Proceed as if you expect your opponents to show up an hour later with the rest of the information that you should have provided. You will have only one opportunity to embarrass a member of Congress or his key staff. If your facts are inadequate, incorrect, incomplete, or selective, don't bother to go back a second time – you won't be welcome.

Even less desirable as visitors, and certainly less effective as lobbyists, are those who forego a professional rollout of the facts in favor of launching into threats of political reprisals for wrong-way votes. Few members are cowed by such a blatant approach. If there is an implied political message, your representative will read it very clearly without being backed into a corner. Tact usually goes further toward achieving a meeting of the minds in Washington than strong-arm methods.

Win with the facts. You *can* do it. Take the case of a Chicago housing developer who got pinned between the courts and Congress.

Bill Alter had won a multimillion-dollar verdict in US district court against the Lake County, Ill., county commissioners by convincing a jury that he had been illegally denied a permit to build in the county. He had proposed lower-cost housing than the officials considered appropriate for this wealthy area of suburban Chicago.

While Lake County was appealing the verdict, a bill that would have voided it automatically was being propelled through Congress by the National League of Cities and the US Conference of Mayors. It stipulated, with a retroactive clause, that cities and counties are exempt from liability under antitrust legislation – which was the basis of Bill Alter's suit.

The bill had passed the House and was ready to roll through the

Senate without major opposition when Alter's counsels, Stuart Eizenstat and Richard Moe, got into the case. Lacking the time to elevate the issue to a generic rather than a personal cause, they went to Senator Howard Metzenbaum (D, Ohio), an original cosponsor of the bill along with Senator Strom Thurmond (R, SC), who was at that time chairman of the Judiciary Committee.

Metzenbaum, a lawyer, saw the irony of having an individual's court decision vacated by the national legislature and agreed to stand up for Alter. He went so far as to tell Thurmond that he couldn't support the bill unless this particular case was taken care of. Thurmond then compromised, not by totally exempting pending cases, but by including guidance to the courts. The guidance stated very clearly that cases already decided by jury verdict should not be overturned.

Case study: discord over the Concorde

In 1975, when France and Great Britain applied for United States landing rights for their jointly developed supersonic passenger plane, the Concorde, they encountered more opposition in Washington than the British Army did in 1812. As a public policy issue, the Concorde's negatives seemed to be overwhelming: in a bitter battle, Congress had just refused to authorize funds for development of the country's own faster-than-sound passenger aircraft, and environmentalists were organized in 435 districts to label Charles DeGaulle's dream a nightmare of noise, dirt, and air pollution which had no redeeming features for anyone other than jet-setters.

When word of organized opposition reached Whitehall and the Quai d'Orsay, the partners determined out of economic necessity to overcome any obstacles that would keep the Concorde from becoming a regular commuter on the profitable North Atlantic route to New York – the only commercial run that would allow them to recoup their huge investment. Their sole supporter was the US Department of State, which surely would not want to estrange such close and cooperative allies, and pledged itself to lobby for the landing rights.

Russell E. Train, administrator of the Environmental Protection Agency, got the battle under way in March 1975 by announcing that limited supersonic traffic at New York's JFK and Washington's

Dulles airports would not pose a real danger to the environment. Train advised President Gerald Ford that the Concordes already constructed should be allowed to land, but that future models should be required to incorporate major sound-reductions. Simultaneously, the Federal Aviation Administration, responding to applications from Air France and British Airways, gave limited approval for Concorde passenger service to Dulles and JFK to begin early in 1976. Noise pollution and environmental impact would be minimal, said the FAA.

The environmental lobby had reached the peak of its influence in 1975. Its grassroots issues held strong appeal for Americans, and its attractive spokesmen, Paul Newman and Robert Redford, movingly projected quality-of-life benefits of clean air and water and pristine public lands. Its power was so great, Concorde lobbyist John Martin Meek recalls, that "you had to have an environmental impact statement to dig a hole in the street, almost."

The Environmental Defense Fund, organized in all congressional districts, was well supplied with vocal voters who were ready to tell their legislators to oppose landings in New York and Virginia. The EDF also knew a lively public issue when it saw one – and the Concorde qualified, in spades.

The best place to stop the Concorde was, of course, where it would hurt France and Britain most: the runways at JFK. Dulles, as a federally run property, was a lost cause for effective citizen action. The huge New York airport, however, was more vulnerable, being under local political control and operated by the Port Authority of New York and New Jersey. Citizens' groups organized immediately, encouraged by local congressmen, governors, and mayors. For months the environmentalists had the field to themselves, inflaming public opinion. Their charges were spread – mostly unanswered – across the newspapers, pictures of middle-class protestors appeared on TV, and London and Paris residents were widely quoted as suffering from sonic booms and toxic emissions.

New Yorkers were sure of responsive political support from their own officials. The Port Authority, concerned about legal liability for problems Concorde overflights and landings might cause the folks on the ground near JFK, told New York governor Hugh Carey that the SST would not be allowed to land until it met all noise and other legal requirements. There were rumors around New York that the

Concorde would rattle dishes like a poltergeist, that the noise of its landings would penetrate the thickest walls, and that the effluent would ruin the ozone layer.

Matters got worse. On July 1, 1975, the Concorde's manufacturers were told that in just 10 days the House would vote on a measure setting noise standards for SSTs – the equivalent of a death certificate for the Concorde in the United States. The legislative champion on the side of the environmentalists was Representative Sidney Yates (D, Ill.). Representative John McFall (D, Cal.), the majority whip, led the forces defending the Concorde.

Before the vote, Yates railed against the "outrageous, earsplitting noise" and discomfort to residents. McFall, briefed by the State Department, cited the potential diplomatic fallout from a ban. He argued that noise charges had not been substantiated, and urged Congress to trust the EPA to protect the environment. McFall won the round, 214–196. The Senate version was a closer thing, losing by only two votes.

Defeat in Congress triggered the flow of even more adrenalin in New York. A split over tactics resulted in the formation of two opposition groups where previously there had been only one. The Emergency Coalition to Stop SST favored political and legal action, whereas the more militant Concorde Alert preferred public demonstrations. When Secretary of Transportation William Coleman announced that he would allow flights on a 16-month trial basis, both groups escalated the battle far beyond nasty letters to *The New York Times*.

More than 1,200 residents of Nassau and Queens counties showed up in Cedarhurst, Long Island, to listen to strategies and oratory by congressmen and local politicians. Mailgrams to be sent to Governor Carey were sold at $2 each, and bumper strips and buttons went for $1. Cards addressed to Air France and British Airways, threatening a boycott "as long as you insist on imposing the Concorde on the US," were also provided.

The Concorde sorely needed a pro-SST constituency in order to balance the news. Its manufacturers assigned a New York public relations company to locate people who would speak up for the big bird. Soon, New Yorkers and the nation were reading that the New York visitors' bureau considered the Concorde a boon to tourism, that the stagnant real-estate market in the city would be revived because the Concorde's landings would herald renewal for New York as an international center. The climate began to change. The PR team, Ray Josephs and David Levy, found prominent Wall Street financiers to be quoted on the dangers of trying to stop technological change. The stores came up with projected figures for the rise in sale of luxury goods. Hotels and restaurants declared their financial interest and so, most importantly, did the unions that represented the dishwashers, waiters, chambermaids, taxi drivers, and retail workers. Instead of a one-sided barrage, voters had started a dialogue, and Congress – with a sigh of relief – noticed the change.

The New York environmentalists, noting the shift in public opinion, decided on an all-out effort to stop the SST if they had to tie New York into knots in the process. While the country was marking George Washington's birthday, Bruce Levinson, who had created Concorde Alert, launched the first protest motorcade, which blocked all the main roads to JFK for 2½ hours. After that, Sunday protests became part of life in New York and caused a backlash. People who hadn't thought about it much one way or another and were willing to go along with the environmentalists on general principle felt that the pollution of the stalled traffic was worse than anything a fleet of Concordes could bring into New York.

The involvement of New York business and unions was frequently and politely brought to the attention of the Hill by the Concorde lobbyists, who up to this point were armed with nothing but an impressive product and the goodwill of the State Department. Now the pro-Concorde votes on the Hill could be based on the preferences of New York voters and not just affairs of state. The Concorde won vote after vote in Congress over the bodies spread out on the Long Island expressways. Then the Concorde itself got into the act. When French president Valéry Giscard d'Estaing arrived in Washington for his Bicentennial visit, he came, of course, on the Concorde, landing at Andrews Air Force Base under carefully controlled and monitored circumstances. Some observers said that Air Force One was noisier; others charged that the landing was rigged.

When Transportation Secretary Coleman's approved flight-schedule began at Dulles, the lobbyists bused congressmen and staffers out there regularly to observe and hear takeoffs and landings.

The British and French ambassadors, at first reluctant to get into the battle directly, responded to proddings from home and headed for the Hill. They had an advantage over the environmentalists – invitations to parties at their respective embassies, by all odds the most elegant in town, where travelers on the Concorde could extol to senators and representatives the virtues of this wonderful technological breakthrough during dinner conversation.

While the velvet glove was being applied in Washington, British Airways and Air France went to court in New York to challenge the Port Authority's ban. Federal Judge Milton Pollack agreed with their challenge, but his ruling was overturned by the appeals court, which told the Port Authority to close the case by setting noise standards. The authorities were reluctant to announce any set of standards and were cited by Judge Pollack for "excessive and unjustified delay." The appeals court agreed, and said the federal law should prevail. The Concorde would land at JFK.

The first Concorde landed there on October 19, 1977. To the surprise and disappointment of many in the crowd that showed up to watch the event, it was no noisier than other planes. Joe Albergo, an automotive repairman, suspected a low Gallic trick. "It sure sounded like that guy cut out his engines or was gliding in. I think France was duping us," he said. Carole Berman, the Emergency Coalition leader who had counseled moderation through most of the battle, conceded that the plane had not been noisier than conventional craft, but noted that it had carried no passengers or cargo. The next morning the Concorde made its first takeoff from New York. As it rose over the water, it made a left turn over the spot where Carole Berman was waiting, strategically placed, with about 100 reporters and a noise meter.

"Here comes the Concorde!" she said. It sailed by with virtually no noise. The last word was spoken by Alan Sagner, chairman of the Port Authority: "For goodness sakes, the damn thing didn't even trip our noise meters."

The very, very last word was spoken by President Jimmy Carter, who had inherited the problem with the job and who had to decide whether or not to make all the landing rights permanent. Carter had campaigned against the Concorde in 1976, but he learned quickly that it is easier to oppose the British and the French out of office than in. In a Solomon-like stance, he gave a half-hour audience to advocates for each side. After weighing the facts, he signed the bill that would let the SST land anywhere in the United States.

Speaking with One Voice

A lobbyist who has been delegated to present an issue on Capitol Hill should not be second-guessed while at work. Any dissension about approaches, goals, or allowable compromises should be kept as far away from the capital as possible. Dissension sends confusing messages to Washington, which is confused enough without it.

A clear case of the importance of eliminating potential quarrels in advance, and of protecting a lobbyist's position as the authoritative representative of a group, came when a tax break won by the nation's retailers in President Reagan's 1981 tax bill came under attack in 1982.

The retailers had lobbied for three years to get faster depreciation for department-store buildings, but no sooner had they gained their goal than the pendulum began to swing against them. Senator Robert Dole, chairman of the Senate Finance Committee, was the central figure in a powerful combination of Senate Finance and House Ways and Means members who were hunting for loopholes in the 1981 tax cut that could be closed to raise revenues. The retailers' prize fitted this category neatly.

While lobbying to keep the provision from going up in smoke, the lobbyist for the National Retail Merchants Association, Verrick O. French, realized that Dole had no personal commitment to the building depreciation issue. As far as the chairman was concerned, French found, it could be retained or sacrificed. Horse trading might be possible.

French worked out a radical approach. Aware that Dole needed support from the business community to get his new tax bill through the Senate, the lobbyist planned a trade-off that would both help the chairman and protect the retailers' depreciation. Under his plan, NRMA would become the first major business-group to endorse the tax bill and actively lobby for it nationally when it emerged from the Finance Committee – without a change in the rules for retail buildings, naturally.

The very idea of lobbying for increased taxes was such a departure from NRMA's procedures that French knew he had to build a consensus in the industry before approaching anyone on the Hill. He lobbied the 22 members of the associations tax committee one at a time, because he knew it would never survive a general discussion. When he had a majority on his side, he called a meeting of the committee. French asked for and got permission to propose the swap to Dole.

The senator proved to be willing. In the closing hours of the committee debate and, more importantly, on the Senate floor, Dole resisted a proposal to dump retail-building depreciation. As promised, the retailers, important constituents in every state, went to bat for passage of the bill in the full Senate without a major amendment. It passed on a 50–47 vote.

French's major achievement had been to gain consensus from his own group on goals and permissible compromises before going to Congress. When a lobbyist fails to do this, the congressional sponsor – the horse – may abandon the cause in frustration. That's what almost happened when 11 trade associations couldn't agree on a goal with respect to a mortgage issue in the Garn-St Germain Depository Institutions Act of 1982. Two of the associations, the US League of Savings Institutions and the National Association of Realtors, had sharply differing views about what should happen to a mortgage when the owner sells a house. The savings and loans wanted to eliminate all assumable mortgages – which can be sold to home buyers without a change in interest rate – partly because of the credit risks associated with them, but mainly to retire low-interest loans as quickly as possible. The realtors, in contrast, liked assumable mortgages, because they are good sales tools. The other associations followed the lead of the Big Two on the issue, and the two teams faced off like bare-knuckle prizefighters right in the Capitol.

After listening to the squabble for months, the bill's sponsor, Senator Jake Garn, then chairman of the Senate Banking Committee, decided enough was enough. "I called them all together," Garn recalls, "and said, 'I can't solve this problem.'"

"There was no way it could have been solved if either side got its own way completely. So I told them, 'You need each other. The realtors can't sell houses without the mortgages, and there won't be mortgages for the thrifts without the sales. I'm not going to attend another meeting with you until you work out a compromise.'"

The 11 groups did just that. Their compromise proposal left to the lender the decision as to whether to include a "due-on-sale" clause in a mortgage but encouraged lenders, in nonbinding language, to negotiate a "blended" mortgage with buyers who wanted to assume the sellers' mortgages. FHA and VA mortgages remained assumable.

"When they brought it back to me," Garn remembers, "I said, 'I want it in writing – a letter to the committee saying that these are terms which you have agreed upon.' And they all signed it."

Showing Flexibility and a Willingness to Compromise

Lobbying is often the art of compromise, so the group you represent must agree in advance on what would be an acceptable result. And you'll need some flexibility to make a deal. John Dingell says that Washington is "full of people who want pie-in-the-sky when they could have pie on the table by accepting a compromise."

Compromise usually offers the only way to get anything done amid a welter of competing interests. The trick is to recognize the best deal when it comes along.

North Dakota environmentalists, fiercely opposing a federal irrigation project that would wipe out 70,000 acres of the best waterfowl-breeding grounds outside Alaska, held fast until they were offered a six-month reprieve and assurance of a full-scale modification study. They made the deal. The alternative was a steamroller, because they were standing in the way of final passage of a $15.4 billion omnibus bill for energy and water projects. How a few people in a thinly populated state could develop the muscle to bargain successfully with the whole US Senate is a good example of the way Washington works.

The Dakota birders were aware that in this case they couldn't even count on their own senators, who were committed to the project. So they brought their problem to the National Audubon Society, which has 500,000 members linked in a vigilant national grassroots network, plus the practical experience so important for effective political action. Promptly, senators in 49 other states who would just as soon stay out of local problems not their own were told by their own constituents that they should vote for the Dakota waterfowl. Enough senators took the matter seriously enough to make the sponsors of the energy and water bill deal with the Dakota problem promptly, so that the omnibus bill could start moving again. Ironically, North Dakota senator Mark Andrews, the irrigation project's principal supporter, finally hammered out the compromise agreement with the Audubon Society.

Another method of flexible lobbying involves knowing parliamentary and congressional rules cold and having a sponsor who is willing to get them enforced. When Mobil tried to buy Ohio's Marathon Oil in an unfriendly takeover, the Ohio delegation in Congress raced to the floor to protect a constituent company by placing a moratorium on mergers and acquisitions. This gave Marathon time to mount a counteroffensive. Marathon's legislative counsel was Tommy Boggs, who had learned congressional maneuvering by osmosis: his father served in Congress, and his mother still does. A bill sponsored by John Dingell in support of the Ohio delegation passed the House under suspension of the rules, without going through a single committee. From there it went straight to the Senate floor – again without being considered by a committee.

But when the majority leader asked if there were any objections, 12 senators spoke up. Their objections had to be satisfied before any action could be taken. It required fast footwork by the Marathon team, because the Christmas recess was imminent, and all bets would be off after a two-week hiatus. Just before the deadline, all the objectors except Senator Howell Heflin (D, Ala.), had been persuaded to change their minds. Boggs hoped that when the Senate returned in January, even Heflin would agree – but he never had a chance to find out. During the Christmas recess, US Steel showed up as a white knight and rescued Marathon through a friendly takeover.

Part III
Orchestrating the Theme

8

Winning at a Hearing

There are two kinds of congressional hearings: investigative hearings, in which witnesses are essentially the targets; and legislative hearings, in which the witnesses bring their expertise to Congress to help the members decide how to handle a national issue. The two types are very different – but both require a great deal of preparation.

Preparing for a Hearing

If you are invited to be a witness at a relevant congressional hearing – and you're in a position to make a public appearance without having to wear a paper bag fitted with eye slits – grab the opportunity. If you haven't been invited, pull strings to get an invitation. Congressional hearings offer the bulliest pulpit in the United States outside of the Oval Office.

A hearing offers an unrivaled chance to publicize your case. Even the most arcane subjects explored on the Hill are reported in detail in some segment of the press – a trade publication, an industry newsletter, your hometown newspaper, or your opposition's broadsides.

"The legislators are not the only listeners at a hearing," says Lynn Greenwalt of the National Wildlife Federation, who encourages his members to testify at appropriate hearings. "If we do it right, the media from the area the witnesses are from are all over the hearing room. It's beamed on TV right back to the home state. No senator or congressman is going to risk not being at the hearing, or making a decision that his constituents object to persuasively. If we've got a case in the media, we've got a case in Congress."

Short of a fistfight on the floor (which has been known to happen), hearings show Congress at its theatrical best. The midget plunked on J. P. Morgan's lap by a press agent in a Senate Banking Committee hearing room in 1933 had nothing to do with the case – but the photo in the next day's papers is all that anybody remembers about the time the great banker came to Washington. Hearings are also Congress's most useful fact-finding forum. While Joe McCarthy's nasal "point of order, Mr Chairman, point of order!" at the celebrated hearings in the 1950s may have been a staple of early TV, the substance of the hearings is well remembered, too. The live broadcasts persuaded the country, as well as McCarthy's colleagues, that there was no basis for the senator's red-baiting charges.

More recently, the Watergate hearings were at least as good as an Agatha Christie thriller in dramatic terms, and they managed to pinpoint, in Senator Howard Baker's words, what the President knew and when he knew it. And still more recently, the sight of a Marine officer in full uniform ducking behind the Fifth Amendment in the Iran-Contra case beat any spy novel hollow.

The hearing that probes your cause may not be quite so historic, but the attention it gets from the people who will have to legislate on the basis of what they learn during this session will be just as intense. Therefore, the preparation of testimony has to be as careful as the crafting of a courtroom brief. You won't be reading the full text at the hearing, but the text will become part of the record, and the record will be pored over carefully.

Coaching witnesses and preparing testimony, including the abstracts and the press information that must be ready before the session, has become one of Washington's growth industries. Some major law firms operate all-night print shops for just such purposes. Practice sessions are as carefully critiqued as performances at acting classes.

That's why you should always get to Washington at least one day before the hearings. You'll then have time to rehearse your position and answer the toughest questions your own team can conjure up in role-playing as senators or congressmen. And besides, if you arrive early you won't have to worry about getting stuck in a traffic jam coming in from the airport and missing your own hearing.

So far, we've been concentrating on *your* agenda. A factor you must always keep in mind is that the hearing has been called by the chairman of the committee, who has his own agenda and his point of view. If your point of view coincides with his – great! If it doesn't, watch out. His very capable staff has been working on this hearing a long time, orchestrating the witnesses and the press. They are as eager to win as you are, and they have the psychological edge – the home court advantage.

The members of the committee sit in high-backed chairs on a dias set in front of a wood-paneled wall. Aides sit behind them, whispering in their ears and slipping them little pieces of paper. The witness sits at a scarred table below the dais, his back to his friends in the audience, and the press and TV lights at his side. It is a very leveling experience, even for the mighty. Every so often a buzzer sounds and the committee members leave the witness in the middle of a sentence to answer a roll call. If they find the witness less than fascinating, they can simply get up and leave – and they often do. The committee chairman has the power of preplanning the sequence of events at his hearing, including the advance publicity.

Under these circumstances, it pays to be ready, whether you will be appearing as a friend or foe of the legislation to be considered. If you are arriving as a friend, be sure that your team has provided, well in advance, questions that can be asked from the chair in order to bring out central points of your argument.

James Fitzpatrick, who takes the lead in prepping witnesses at his law firm, Arnold & Porter, says the most important principle to follow in getting ready for a hearing is the Boy Scout motto, Be Prepared. Beyond this, he offers other rules to live by in such circumstances.

Keep it short No one has ever lost a case in Congress by being too brief. Even if you think your position can't be understood in less than an hour, boil your presentation down to five minutes, maximum, because nobody in Congress has an hour to listen. This is particularly true around lunchtime and late in the day.

Don't read your statement A good salesman never reads from a prepared statement; he talks to you. Once you've condensed your argument to the essential points, practice talking it out *without* looking at your notes. The committee members will have your written statement in front of them anyway.

Don't be arrogant A lot of congressional witnesses get short-tempered because they believe the committee members "don't understand my business." Too bad. Most congressmen don't give a damn whether they understand your business. They are going to make a political decision based on what they hear. A witness should never be gratuitously argumentative.

Don't guess The worst thing you can do is to try to give a specific answer you're not sure about. In an investigative hearing, some member will try to trap you by pinning you down on a fact or statistic you're not sure about. Don't fall for it. If you don't know the answer to a question, tell the chairman that you don't know and that you will supply that answer to the committee later. It is always better to answer correctly later than to answer incorrectly now.

Don't be hokey, but illustrate whenever possible It's easier to focus on a wrecked fender that sits right in the hearing room than to visualize a set of statistics. A group of Mexican vegetable growers, fighting a tariff on their products, wanted to prove that their vegetables came to market riper than the American vegetables that they were competing against – a point difficult to convey in a statement. Then a witness dropped two tomatoes from chest-level in the hearing room. The Mexican tomato splattered all over the plastic the lawyer had carefully placed on the floor, while the American tomato bounced knee-high, like a tennis ball. The committee got the point.

Case Study: Invsco Turns the Tables

With careful preparation and a good presence, even the most severely grilled witness can come out looking good. Take the experience of Nick Gouletas, chairman of American Invsco, who was called before Congress to show that his corporation was not grinding the faces of the elderly poor.

In 1980, Invsco, the largest condominium conversion company in the country, came under severe and very public criticism. According to detractors, the company was unfairly dispossessing older people who could not afford the considerable down payment necessary to purchase the apartment they were living in after Invsco bought their buildings.

Two days before Nick Gouletas's appearance before a subcommittee, *60 Minutes* carried a devastating segment on the company's condominium conversion policies, alleging that its practices had unfairly evicted many tenants. There was little likelihood of a coincidence in timing between the two events, because the subcommittee chairman, the late Representative Benjamin Rosenthal (D, NY), was a fierce supporter of affordable rental housing for the middle class, as well as a congressman known and liked by the media.

Rosenthal ostensibly had called the hearings to explore the adequacy of federal laws governing the conversion of apartments into condominiums. In fact, however, the congressman considered Invsco the flagship of the enemy, and he intended to use the hearings to sink it. To do so, he needed national exposure of the basis of the case – and he got just that from *60 Minutes*.

Because Gouletas by himself would have little chance of surviving Rosenthal's determined questioning, the company's Washington lawyers arranged some help for him. Their plan was that Gouletas would appear flanked by two distinguished consultants: Andrew Brimmer, a former governor of the Federal Reserve Board and now the head of a major economic research analysis firm, and Thomas (Lud) Ashley, a lawyer who had been Congress's leading authority on housing during his 20 years as a representative from Toledo.

A group of us had prepped Nick most of the night at the Arnold & Porter offices by tossing him what we thought would be Rosenthal's toughest questions: "Didn't you send an eviction notice to a woman in a wheelchair whose husband was dying?" "Didn't you sell apartments out from under the elderly people who rented them but could not afford to buy them?"

Gouletas glowered at the beginning, but he had the good sense to realize that he would have to keep his temper when the chairman asked such provocative questions. And he knew that having heard the questions in advance, he would find them easier to handle the next day.

The hearing-room was jammed an hour before the kickoff with the pencil press, network camera crews, photographers, and flocks of retired renters. All expected to watch Invsco's demise. But they received a surprise. Gouletas turned out to be a very astute and appealing witness.

Ashley spoke first, addressing substantive issues of housing. Because this was his first appearance as a witness before Congress since leaving the House, the entire subcommittee was on hand to honor an esteemed former colleague.

It was nearly noon when Ashley and Brimmer were through and Gouletas was ready to begin. He came across as a very reasonable and public-spirited businessman – the very image of the American dream, a poor Greek immigrant who had come to the United States and become successful. He finished his prepared statement by thanking the committee and saying how much he appreciated the opportunity to appear before Congress.

"It shows that democracy works," Gouletas concluded.

Rosenthal smiled and looked at Jim Fitzpatrick, who was at Gouletas' side throughout the hearing. "It works particularly well when you have an excellent law firm like Arnold & Porter to help get you prepared," Rosenthal pointed out.

During the questioning, Gouletas never allowed Rosenthal to get the upper hand. When Rosenthal demanded to know what Invsco was doing to handle complaints, Nick responded by saying that the company had hired an ombudsman who had once worked for the B'nai Brith – and Rosenthal could do nothing but agree with the wisdom of that choice! When Rosenthal charged that Invsco's practices could be in violation of securities law, Nick quietly reminded him that the Securities & Exchange Commission had already informed the committee that no law had been broken.

The congressman from New York hardly laid a glove on the enemy, and American Invsco later had more trouble with 18 percent interest rates than it ever had with the subcommittee.

The outcome of congressional hearings may often be in the laps of the gods, but you've got a better chance of landing in a comfortable lap if you are well prepared.

9

Working with the Media

Nothing is more influential in Washington than a page 1 story in the *Washington Post, The New York Times,* or the *Wall Street Journal* – except, of course, a series of stories on the same subject. *Your* chances of coming up with a front-page story to back a lobbying effort are rather slim. But if your issue involves a lot of money, affects a lot of people, or involves a threat to the quality of life, it will probably fit somewhere in a metropolitan newspaper.

High visibility can have a wildfire effect on legislation, provided that the newsmaker is as thorough and as credible as Robert S. McIntyre. One of the most successful movers and shakers in Washington in 1986, McIntyre wielded his power not with a sword or a pen, but with a computer. While hundreds of lobbyists were trying to mold the Tax Reform Act to their own specifications, McIntyre exercised the greatest influence on the shape of the mammoth bill, without going near a congressman. He worked exclusively through the news media.

A public-interest tax lawyer whose idea of heaven is to curl up with a stack of corporate annual reports, McIntyre announced at a press conference that 130 of the nation's biggest companies had been using a loophole in the Internal Revenue code to avoid paying any income taxes at all from 1981 through 1985, even though they had earned a collective $72.9 billion. The resultant public outcry placed the issue on the congressional tax agenda just a few weeks later.

McIntyre, who works for a low-budget nonprofit organization supported principally by labor, was his own chief researcher and his own public relations man for the report he was preparing. He gave equal thought to both aspects as he painstakingly gathered evidence of corporate tax loopholes in his cluttered fourth-floor K Street walk-up office at the Citizens for Tax Justice, one of dozens of obscure public-interest watchdog groups listed in the Washington telephone directory. Very few people look up these numbers, but most of those who do are reporters. And once a reporter got a tax briefing from Bob McIntyre, the number went onto his or her Rolodex promptly, for McIntyre is a prime specimen of that mysterious figure in American journalism known as a "reliable source."

The experts employed by public-interest groups – in nutrition, environment, taxes, health, and a dozen other categories – are generally well-regarded by the Washington media. The stories they offer are provocative and make good copy. These experts also usually have time to talk to reporters, which they enjoy doing because it gives them visibility, which in turn helps them to gain funding and to find new contributors.

McIntyre had made many friends in the media over his seven years in Washington by making himself available to interpret and comment on arcane tax matters that reporters have to turn into understandable English under deadline pressure. Although he was almost as unknown to the public and Congress as he had been upon coming to Washington seven years before to work for Ralph Nader, he had established his credibility with a wide swath of reporters.

So when he had a story of his own that was so basic and so incredible that even the Democratic chairman of the House Ways and Means Committee might have considered it outlandish, the reporters were not only ready to listen – they could also reassure their editors that he was an authority and that his facts would hold up under close scrutiny.

He also timed his announcement correctly. The President's tax bill was being rushed to completion at the Treasury Department, and through friends over there he kept tabs on its progress. McIntyre carefully scheduled his press conference so it fell one week ahead of the delivery of the tax-reform bill to Congress. That was the vehicle that could do something about curing the problem he was identifying.

McIntyre orchestrated his big story like a sunrise. Headlines blared the news, while long articles in newspapers across the country named the prominent companies that had gotten away scot-free on taxes. Angry editorials quickly followed, and the reaction on the Hill led directly to the plugging of the loopholes in the new law. That's effectiveness in Washington.

Setting the Agenda

Public issues thrive on ink or die from the lack of it, and the daily competition for the attention of the news media in Washington is fierce. So the decision of how and when to break a story is crucial. The rewards can be great because – the protests of editors that they are just covering the news notwithstanding – the media dictate the agenda in the capital. The politician hasn't been born who relishes working on projects that don't command public attention. And public attention comes with news reports.

Mo Udall, the long-time representative from Arizona, told us that an editorial, a news story, or an interesting op-ed piece in one of the major papers will have the Hill talking about it at least from breakfast through lunch. That factor greatly amplifies the effectiveness of one-on-one lobbying.

And the Hill isn't the only place where the heavyweight papers are being read. Scouts for the *MacNeil/Lehrer News Hour* and the morning TV news programs mine the papers for ideas and sources. The wire services and the Washington bureaus of the newspapers back home pick up stories and spread them across America. And all the network news programs follow the lead of the national papers on many stories.

Thus, it's possible that a legislator will read about an issue in the morning paper in Washington, hear it discussed in the House gym at lunchtime, and see it on TV while he's shaving the next day. He may then get a copy of another story about it in the mail from a constituent, find it featured and editorialized in his hometown paper, and see it embellished by his favorite columnist and recapped in *Time* and *Newsweek* the following Monday morning. That kind of exposure makes any issue hard to ignore. Legislators may be for it or against it or have no opinion whatsoever, but they certainly will be aware of it. Then, too, with all that public exposure the constituency for the issue will start to grow.

Conversely, just one well-timed story can sink a perfectly executed lobbying effort overnight. As mentioned earlier, a dispatch from Tokyo in the *Washington Post* and *The New York Times* 24 hours before a key vote changed the course of the so-called Toshiba amendment to the 1988 trade bill and possibly cost the Japanese company as much as $130 million a year in its business with the United States.

Reaching the right audiences

Every newspaper, magazine, TV or radio network, and trade publication of any size has a Washington office. That goes not only for the US media, but also for the Japanese, Indian, French, German, British, and Chinese as well. Those lacking their own bureaus are represented by news services that cover Washington with an eye to local impact for the client. The offices range in size from the cavernous newsrooms of big bureaus and the TV networks down to one-man operations.

According to the most recent count made by Howard Hudson, who publishes an indispensable annual directory of the Washington press, there are 3,426 news outlets in Washington, staffed by approximately 8,000 reporters. Except for those who work on purely local beats, any one of these reporters could be a factor in the work you do in Washington. They talk not only to official Washington, but also to the people back home who do the voting.

Choosing your words

One of the greatest threats to success in Washington is saying more than is necessary. The town is a veritable sieve, and even pillow talk – unless it is with a mate of many years who isn't likely to start divorce proceedings – can show up in the media next week. The ground rules for interviews that seem to imply rules of conduct – "off the record," "background briefing," "deep background," etc. – immediately become inoperative when you utter something unexpected that is worth printing. The only rule to follow is, *If you don't want the whole world to know it the next day, don't say it.*

Winning in Washington depends directly on audience-specific communication. Bob McIntyre's Citizens for Tax Justice wanted each and every member of the Ways and Means Committee to hear not from them, but from outraged citizens, while the committee was still in the early stages of debate. Among the truly outraged would be executives of many big businesses that had been shelling out their fair share of taxes while competitors were benefiting from the break. Widespread publicity got the story across to the right audience.

Using signed articles (op-eds) effectively

Important messages in Washington are also delivered through the media to much smaller audiences – in fact, to as few as one or two people. Before springing a new idea, the White House often tests reaction by leaking little notes to Congress attributed to a "senior administration official." The Speaker of the House doesn't dip a quill into an inkwell to answer – he calls a press conference. If the idea doesn't fly, the press is blamed for listening to poorly informed leakers, and the administration can disavow any connection with an unworkable plan.

It is sometimes easier for a leader to plant an idea or bury a hatchet with a well-written 800-word op-ed piece in the morning paper than to invite the opposition to a meeting. In Washington, ideas arrive with the breakfast coffee.

Senator Bob Dole used this means of communication when he wanted to let the Democrats on the Senate Finance Committee, which he chaired, know that the Republicans were ready to negotiate the end of a long-standing Social Security impasse.

The future of the Social Security system had been front-page news from the moment President Reagan took office in 1981. The system was in financial trouble, and no solution was in sight. The White House wanted to convert Social Security into a voluntary pension fund. The Democrats, led by Senator Daniel Patrick Moynihan (D, NY), believed that the fund was basically healthy and only needed some fine-tuning. Squarely in the middle were the Republican senators, led by Dole, who were charged with supporting a presidential position that wasn't going to play in Peoria or Portland.

Following a time-honored presidential custom for dealing with problems that have no easy solutions, President Reagan appointed a blue-ribbon commission, which met for a year and ended in a stalemate. The Republicans on the commission filed a majority report, the Democrats filed a minority report, and by the end of 1982 the issue was still unresolved. Social Security still seemed to be at risk, and the country was concerned.

So Dole wrote a signed article for the *Washington Post*, a so-called op-ed piece, or guest editorial. (In compositor talk, op-ed stands for the page opposite the editorial page.) In his piece, Dole said that he believed the problem could be fixed and, furthermore, that he thought President Reagan would be amenable to a solution.

Dole's article appeared on the opening day of the 1983 session of the Senate. Moynihan, who had arrived in Washington that morning to be sworn in for his second term, got the hint immediately. At the swearing-in ceremony, he asked Dole whether he meant what he had written. Dole said he did.

The two of them started meeting privately the same day and then quickly expanded the group to include a few other key players who had to be part of any acceptable solution: James A. Baker 3rd, then the White House chief of staff; House Speaker Tip O'Neill (D, Mass.); Representative Barber Conable (R, NY), representing the House Republicans; AFL-CIO president Lane Kirkland; and several specialists.

In 12 days of nonofficial talks that moved from a Senate back room to Jim Baker's rumpus room to the elegant drawing room of Blair House, the presidential guest house, they hammered out a compromise agreement that was accepted by the President and became the Social Security Amendment of 1983. It took just 45 minutes to get the amendment through the House Ways and Means Committee – a new speed record for a committee that usually takes nine months to review even the least controversial legislation. Moynihan says that the appearance of Dole's article in the *Post* – the right message in the right place at the right time – was distinctly the catalyst. "It was as if he had left a note on the bulletin board for me," the senator recalls.

Obviously, Senator Dole starts off with a distinct advantage over the average lobbyist when he submits a signed piece to the editor. But you can do exactly the same thing – if not in the *Washington Post*, at least in the hometown papers of the members of the right congressional committees. The principal requirements are that the issue be of real interest to a large portion of the readership and that the editorial be both timely and well-written.

Getting Your Story Across

The basic point to grasp in working with the news media is that reporters are in the business of purveying news stories and are constantly in need of a fresh supply. If you have a good story to offer and you present it well, it will carry itself.

Take the example of Jan Scruggs and a few other Vietnam veterans who were doggedly covering the Hill trying to gain support for a national Vietnam War Memorial on the Mall – a monument to their fallen comrades and also a symbol of the healing of the rift between those who had gone to Vietnam to fight and those who had gone to Capitol Hill to stop the war.

Scruggs and his colleagues had the enthusiastic support of senators such as Charles Mathias (R, Md) and John Warner (R, Va.), as well as almost everyone else they went to see. The papers duly noted their progress, and official approval was assured. What they didn't have was funding. Since there was no line item in the budget for a Vietnam War Memorial, the project needed national attention. We were given the assignment.

The situation was tailor-made for a nationally syndicated columnist. James J. Kilpatrick, one of the nation's leading conservative columnists, was given the first look at the story. He thought the Vietnam Veterans Memorial Fund was important, and he wrote a moving column about it that appeared in hundreds of newspapers. For the first time in his career, Kilpatrick included an appeal for donations and a mailing address for a fund. In less than two weeks, Scruggs had a nest egg of $187,000, contributed in small amounts from people all around the country, with which to launch the successful campaign that resulted in the Vietnam Veterans Memorial – perhaps the most haunting and beautiful memorial in all of Washington.

Many people today have a good grasp of media relations. The hearing-impaired students at federally funded Gallaudet University, the nation's only liberal-arts university for the deaf, knew in their bones that they needed major exposure on TV and in the newspapers to turn the tide in their battle with the institution's board of directors. They wanted a university president who could understand, from experience, the problems of being deaf. Instead, the board of directors appointed an educator who was fully qualified in every aspect except for fluency in sign language – the only way to communicate face-to-face with the student body. When the word got out, the students promptly hit the bricks.

The Washington newspapers and TV stations were brought into the picture right away by Greg Hlibok, the student-body president. They were kept fully informed as the protest developed, first on the campus and then in a march through the streets of the capital aiming at delivering a blow to the university's midsection at the source of its funding – the United States Congress. Local and network TV cameras, along with print reporters, followed the march step by step as the protestors rallied at the Capitol and brought their story to the two congressmen on the board of Gallaudet. Board Chairman Jane Bassett Spilman, who had said the board would stick with its decision despite the protest, was beginning to come across to the public like the director of the orphanage in *Annie*.

The coup de grâce for Ms Spilman was self-inflicted. Once the media was invited in, every move in the drama had to be played out in its glare, and Ms Spilman had the misfortune to try to address a noisy assembly of students with 60 TV cameras following the action.

"If you make all that noise, I can't hear you," she exclaimed through her interpreter, as every camera in the room turned on the students, who were shrugging and signing, "What noise?"

The new president, whom Gary Hlibok called a victim who didn't know what she was getting into, resigned the following day. The board's next appointment met all the requirements, and the victorious students went happily back to their books.

If yours is less than a world-shaking issue, you can still rivet the attention of the media, but you may have to be ingenious about it. We remember the woman who showed up at Andrews Air Force Base with a huge sign reading "Hello Luxembourg!" The only problem was that she was presumably there to greet the Prince of Wales, who was arriving for a state visit. Even the Prince noted the incongruity when he did a walkabout and shook hands over the fence.

"Why does your sign say 'Hello Luxembourg' instead of 'Hello Charles'?" he asked. And the woman said, "I knew this would be on television on the *Armed Forces Network* and I thought I might say hello to my cousin who is stationed in Luxembourg."

Finding a Local News Slant

On a scale of 1 to 10, lobbyist Tommy Boggs estimates that hometown papers rate a 9 in terms of influencing a legislator, whereas the national papers and television news programs come up no higher than a 6 or a 7. So, like salesmen with sample cases, lobbyists also have to carry their ideas to the media back home.

One of the most successful media grassroots programs of recent years was conducted by a coalition called AutoChoice. The core of its small membership was composed of General Motors and Ford, which had decided to take to the country the case for lowering the Corporate Fuel Economy standards (CAFE) from 27.5 miles per gallon to 26. This position was opposed by Chrysler, which was happily producing mostly small cars. With the help of the E. Bruce Harrison Co., GM and Ford executives went from city to city and state to state, generating news and favorable editorials that sang of Americans' love affair with big cars and the problems caused by unrealistic standards.

Each visit had a local angle, because the auto manufacturers were joined by neighborhood car dealers. It was a thorough, time-intensive program. The Department of Transportation took due note of the two volumes of supporting editorials, which had also been sent to congressional offices, and lowered the standards.

A national story *must* have a local angle to be of interest in a grassroots media tour. For a trade issue: How many jobs depend on it right here in River City? For a public project: How much money will flow into the area as a result? For a tax bill: How will it affect the local industries; the general population?

Many companies and trade groups employ field representatives whose sole duty is to ride the circuit and call on the media in specific regions. The public relations director at one large association, who served his time as a legman and now supervises a field force, says that the most important ingredient of success is understanding that the editor's agenda is not the same as the agenda of the Washington representative who is peddling the story.

"Things that seem to be of real importance in Washington, coming up just over the horizon, often don't have the same urgency in Montana or South Dakota," he says. "Time and again, I'd get out there and be told, 'It's not news here yet. Come back when they're ready to vote'."

Senator Jake Garn makes the same observation from another viewpoint. "When I lose on an issue in Washington after a tough battle, it seems the most important and agonizing thing that has ever happened," he says. "Then I get off the plane in Salt Lake City and ask people about it, and they never even heard of it."

Tactics and Pitfalls

It is no easy matter to break into the evening news or the morning paper. Each week the *Washington Post*'s editorial department receives 5,000 unsolicited written communications from all over the world – everything from social tidbits for the Style section to press releases about new products and the promotion of new corporate vice-presidents aimed at the business section. Every bit of it gets sorted and scanned.

About 90 percent of these items don't survive the scanning processes. Here are some professional tips to help you survive the first cut in the daily editorial triage at any big city paper.

Make the news fit to print The paper's only duty is to print what its editors perceive to be news. Therefore, your job is to make your material as newsworthy as you possibly can. For example, the projected worldwide devastation from acid rain in the year 2097 is not going to excite many editors as potential news tomorrow; the threatened wipe-out of all sports fishing in a lake in northern Minnesota next year is a different story, however.

Don't count on friendship Friendship with a reporter will get your telephone calls returned, but will not get a nonstory in the paper. Even if the reporter is your mother and she wants to help you, she will have trouble getting past the editor's desk in the competition for space. There is no substitute for finding angles to your stories that make them news.

Study the media you want to crack Know their various departments, and who their audience is. It's not enough to be the average reader who gulps down Ann Landers and the sports headlines with the danish. You have to anatomically dissect every section in which your story might fit for insights on news value.

• *Don't phone at deadline times* If you do, you'll be starting off with two strikes against you: one, the person has no time to talk to you; and two, she'll be annoyed at the interruption. Make it a practice to begin your conversation by asking, "Are you on deadline?" If the answer is yes, say you've got an interesting story and you'll call at a more convenient time. There is an art to taking advantage of slow periods in Washington. Congressional press secretaries are particularly skilled at these techniques. They can be very creative at the job of keeping their boss's ideas in the papers and on the tube. Terry Smith, now a television correspondent, recalls that when he was an editor in the Washington bureau of *The New York Times,* a particular visitor from the Hill appeared in the newsroom like clockwork every Friday evening. At every visit he would deliver a story about a dreadful fate from which the country had just been saved by the timely intervention of his boss. The press secretary knew that although Washington is a five-day news operation, the papers need material for the sixth and seventh days as well.

Schedule press conferences carefully Press conferences can be a flop in Washington if you don't understand how the town works. In fact, press conferences sometimes can fail even if you do everything right. No matter how large and specialized the press corps becomes, Washington is still a one-story town. If the President decides to make an announcement, or if Congress schedules an important vote, or if it snows more than half an inch, your press conference is likely to fail.

Do not call a press conference unless you have solid, honest-to-goodness news of interest to a wide variety of reporters. A press conference requires busy people to be in a certain place at a certain time to listen to what you have to say. If it isn't important in the general scheme of the day's news, you have lost the confidence of the press corps. They probably won't show up for that second shot when you have a genuine story of enough interest to help your cause.

There are other dangers in a press conference. The most newsworthy of stories can be buried by a sensational event that diverts the entire press corps. We had press conferences scheduled on the days when someone attempted to assassinate the Pope, when the space capsule blew up, when President Sadat was killed. We also had one scheduled for nine o'clock on the morning when the biggest ice-storm of the season paralyzed Washington. As things turned out, that was the only one of the four that didn't flop. We had invited the media to introduce an amazing machine that could scan ordinary print, translate it into sound, and read it back to the blind. It was the first device of its kind, and there had been a good deal of advance interest from the general press, as well as from technical writers in the field.

Things looked disastrous when only one reporter showed up – a delightful elderly lady who lived around the corner from the building where the conference was taking place. As it happened, she was on her last day of work after 40 years with the Associated Press. Her story appeared in virtually every paper in the country, and sales of that machine soared, particularly to government libraries.

If you must hold a press conference, time and place are important. If you think you have a shot at the network or local evening news, plan it no later than the early afternoon; only natural disasters, plane crashes, and crimes of passion can make the TV news production cycle after 4.00 PM. Apart from that, there's no *right* time during the day – there's competition every hour on the hour for the attention of the media. As for place, convenient and well-equipped locations include the National Press Club, the International Club, and – if a congressman will sponsor you – rooms in the Capitol and the congressional office buildings. If you can't get access to a club, downtown hotels will do fine.

Always rehearse your spokesperson. If you are the spokesperson, have somebody pepper you with questions likely to crop up. Remember that, as in a congressional hearing, anything you say goes on the record. Another tip: don't let a press conference go longer than three-quarters of an hour. Whatever the subject, you don't have that much of interest to say, and there aren't enough questions. With all the troubles of the world on his back, the President of the United States ends his conferences in half an hour, and then sometimes makes his biggest headline by answering a reporter's offhand question as he is walking out the door.

When Congress has gone home and the President is weekending at Camp David, reporters write their "Washington insider" books and take their kids to the Smithsonian. So unless you are faced with an emergency, don't let yourself be talked into a weekend press conference. We once wound up in such a situation, and it took the combined experience of a pair of seasoned parents to salvage the situation.

Saturday was the only day that maestro Mstislav Rostropovich, conductor of the National Symphony, could find time for a press conference to introduce a group of 11-year-old virtuosi who were going to play their own compositions as soloists with his orchestra at a Kennedy Center concert. The event was the culmination of a worldwide competition for composers 18 and younger, sponsored by Yamaha, the Japanese piano manufacturer, and it was meant to heighten the corporation's profile in Washington.

Seeking to turn the Saturday problem into an advantage, we lured reporters into coming out on the weekend by inviting them to bring their own children along to question the kids. The event was turned into a picnic, with hot dogs, hamburgers, and a contest for the best story by a junior reporter.

Make press releases focused and accurate Putting irrelevant material on the desks of reporters who have absolutely no interest in it wins a booby prize for you and your issue. Also, scattering press releases all over the place can bring you attention from quarters you'd just as soon not hear from.

Whatever you do, spell the names right. Check and recheck. That goes for "Smith" as well as "Brzezinski." If you make a mistake, you'll lose credibility quickly, not just with the reporters, but with the friendly congressman who has just agreed to be the horse for your issue and can't stand anyone misspelling the name he has been merchandising for the past 20 years.

Tell your story as interestingly as you possibly can. Nobody is going to read a whole page of pedestrian writing that doesn't make a point. Get the most significant part in the lead paragraph. The reader should be able to grasp the nub of the story after finishing the lead.

10

Finding Allies

Building a Coalition

Once you have found even one ally willing to lend a hand, you have formed a legislative coalition. People who join coalitions do so out of enlightened self-interest. If your ox is about to be gored, warn the owners of the other oxen in the neighborhood and fight the threat together. Coalitions create a very useful product called clout. The more interests you can get to stand up for your side, the better the chance that legislators will consider the project. In building coalitions, you'll also be gaining strength in congressional districts where you previously may not have known a soul.

The interests are constantly coalescing and separating in the day-to-day work of winning in Washington. Aware that they can seldom win all by themselves in a complex, interdependent society, effective lobbyists line up whatever allies they can find, and the frequently shifting alliances make for odd bedfellows. The farmers can team up one day with the railroads, their historical sparring partners, to defeat a coal-slurry pipeline proposal – and the next day join another coalition to fight the same railroads on rate hikes. Ralph Nader will oppose big business reflexively every way he can, yet wind up in harness with the major corporations, unions, and public interest groups to beat down attempts to tighten lobbying laws.

Be sure you know who else is fighting for the same issue, and make it a point to be on speaking terms with them, however outlandish that may sound. From 1984 through 1986, industry, labor, and the environmental groups were fighting to push the $20 billion clean-water act through Congress. Since their interests were so disparate, they haggled separately with the government and couldn't muster a veto-proof majority when President Reagan decided that the government couldn't foot the bill for the act.

There the matter stood until someone had the bright idea to call a meeting of the competing interests and shape them into a coalition. Lobbying together, they made the clean-water bill veto-proof, and it became law as the first act to pass Congress in 1987.

The building and running of coalitions is big business in Washington. The Chamber of Commerce of the United States has a special staff whose sole job is to knit different interests together; they form about 80 coalitions a year. Washington's law, lobbying, and public relations firms are constantly doing the same thing for their clients.

If you want to locate prospective allies on your own, just think about who else is going to be helped or hurt by the project occupying your attention. This process demands creative thinking on your part, along with suspension of conventional ideas of who your traditional enemies are.

Once identified, prospective allies must be approached with tact, caution, and pinpointed position papers that explain the issue clearly in terms of *their* self-interest. The motivation can be simple economic necessity, as it was when Chrysler and the United Auto Workers teamed up to fight for the automaker's loan guarantee. Or it can be philosophical reasoning, as it was when the fundamentalist Christian right joined with the Israel lobby to block US arms sales to Jordan.

Getting members to sign up for a coalition is easy. The hard part is getting them to do something besides lending their names to the letterhead. Out of a 50-member coalition, perhaps five will be really active in the day-to-day work of organizing, telephoning, and shoe-leather stalking of Congress on behalf of their cause. Even if all members of a coalition make equal financial contributions at the beginning of a battle, it's likely that only the active members, those who have also put in time and effort, will chip in when the second request for funds goes out.

Ten Rules for a Successful Coalition

Anne Wexler, a specialist in creating legislative coalitions, has identified 10 guidelines for getting them started, keeping them together, and keeping them on track. The only equipment missing from this list are the whip, chair, and riding boots of the professional lion tamer.

1   *Appeal to your prospect's self-interest.* Be sure to identify carefully who will win if your position prevails, who will lose, and who will have reasons to stay neutral.
2   *Be aggressive.* Identify every organization that should be contacted: groups that will be with you, groups that will be against you, and groups whose positions you don't know. Contact each one and keep a record of their priorities and the facts that influence their positions.
3   *Find the activists and put them to work.* Don't just sign up allies. Find out what each member can bring to the effort. Determine who will work hard and who will not, and who needs more information to be effective.
4   *Educate legislators, the public, and yourself.* Learn what the opposition knows. Have an educational strategy of your own and a communication plan to implement it.
5   *Develop consensus.* Get the coalition to reach decisions and perform tasks.
6   *Establish a dialogue with the other side.* Learn their arguments and strive to blunt their criticism – in the hope that you can encourage some of them to remain neutral.
7   *Negotiate.* There must be a willingness to negotiate at any point in the legislative process – first with allies, and then with adversaries – in order to achieve the coalition's goals.
8   *Be open to new ideas.* Stay flexible. Don't miss innovative ideas merely by reacting negatively out of habit.
9   *Know when to compromise.* To be sure that you are around when the final decisions are made, you must know the right time for compromise. Act too soon and

you'll preempt any chance of total victory; wait too
long, and no one will need you.

10   *Maintain your network*. Don't forget your allies once the
battle has been fought and won. Use them at the
grassroots level to enhance your future lobbying efforts.

Case Study: Morgan Stanley Switches Tracks for Conrail

One of the best illustrations of putting the coalition rules into action
was the 1985–6 effort by Morgan Stanley & Co., the investment
banking firm, to stop the Reagan administration from selling the
Consolidated Rail Company (Conrail) to a competing railroad.
Formed by the merger of seven failed or failing railroads in the East
and Midwest, Conrail was owned 85 percent by the government and
15 percent by its employees.

When Conrail started to make money in the 1980s, the Reagan
Administration decided to marry off its railroad to a rich private
suitor, the Norfolk Southern. But Morgan Stanley made a remarkable
11th-hour fight to turn the railroad into a public company of its own.

At the time Secretary of Transportation Elizabeth Dole announced
that Conrail was going to be sold for $1.2 billion, Morgan Stanley
was engaged in a study for Conrail's management on the best options
for returning the railroad to the private sector. Stunned by the
unexpected decision, Morgan Stanley and Conrail's management
challenged the administration. They predicted that such a merger
would eliminate important railroad competition, as well as many
jobs. Morgan Stanley said that Conrail didn't need a new owner –
even one with the great credentials of the Norfolk Southern – and
that it could and should survive as a public company.

Big investors join up

The investment banking firm was so convinced of the wisdom of this
course of action that it decided to put its own money where its report
was. It formed a group of 25 well-financed and prestigious investors
– including several of the Rockefellers, Citibank, and three Ivy

League universities who felt the same way about the future of Conrail.

They presented Secretary Dole with a formal proposal matching the $1.2 billion offer. The proposal called for the investors to serve as caretaker owners for five years until a public stock offering could be packaged. In the meantime, Conrail would continue to be run by the current management. To back its challenge, the company needed high visibility, a strong presence in Washington, and a broad-based coalition. The firm of Wexler, Reynolds, Harrison, and Schule was hired to form and run the coalition.

Their first step was to identify prospective coalition members. The freight shippers were logical allies, since they would feel any loss of rail competition in their pocketbooks. Labor was also an obvious choice; the unions know that mergers mean fewer jobs. And farmers, who move products by rail, historically distrusted merged railroads. Finally, a case for competition and loss of revenue could be made to city governments, and state attorneys general might respond to the antitrust aspects of a major railroad merger at a time when so few companies were left in the field.

Then came the outreach effort. The initial 50 members of a coalition are the most difficult to recruit, because at first people aren't sure they want to be bothered, and there is no list of members to impress them. But Morgan Stanley scored a grand slam with its first recruiting letter. Among the first 50 they managed to sign up were 14 state attorneys general, a handful of governors, and a number of mayors.

When the list reached 100 and the organization clearly was here to stay, a press conference was called to announce that the Coalition for a Competitive Conrail (CCC) had been formed to stop the Norfolk Southern purchase, which needed congressional approval.

After the press conference, everyone on the letterhead was contacted again as chores were parceled out. In this way the organizers quickly were able to distinguish people who just wanted to have their names used from those who were really going to work. It enabled the organizers to build an activist group within the coalition, which began the job of educating and informing legislators and the public.

Economic impact papers were developed for every state on the Conrail line, describing the negative aspects of the takeover. The

Michigan version, for example, pointed out that Conrail's impact on the state's economy "far exceeds the 2,157 Michigan employees and 528 route miles of track in the state," because "many Michigan businesses will be injured if Conrail is eliminated as an independent competitive force." The paper detailed how competition between Conrail and Norfolk Southern had saved Chrysler and General Motors $9–$10 million and Detroit Edison $3.7 million in two years through rate reductions, service innovations, and shipper advocacy programs.

Membership continues to grow

Meanwhile, CCC's membership was growing. Between June and November, it increased from 41 pioneers to 257 individuals and groups. The members were kept united and informed through a newsletter, which served also as a bulletin board for assignments, and were urged to meet with representatives and senators during the August recess, when the latter returned to their home bases.

Articles and editorials inspired by the coalition's public relations operation began to appear. Late in the year, each member of the Senate received a package wrapped in Kraft paper from coalition headquarters with a note saying, "When something arrives in a brown paper wrapper, you'd better look at it carefully." Inside was a Monopoly set with a letter that began, "Monopoly is more than a game." Such aggressive promotions usually make conservative Wall Street investment bankers wince, but the Morgan Stanley partners got into the spirit when it was explained that getting the Hill's attention on any issue – much less one that challenges a popular president, the secretary of transportation, and the latter's husband, the Senate majority leader – requires imaginative approaches.

Legislative order of the day: delay!

The coalition's Hill strategy could have been devised by the Roman general Cunctator, who won his battles by delaying the fight. Bills that would make Conrail a public corporation were introduced early in both chambers, but since the sponsors were aware that they didn't have the votes, the coalition concentrated on slowing the administration's Norfolk Southern bill. The theory was that if enough obstacles were put in the way of the merger, Norfolk Southern's management might get edgy and set a deadline for completion of the deal.

The immediate objective was to prevent the bill from coming to a vote in the Senate, where Secretary Dole would surely win. Senate Commerce Committee Chairman John Danforth (R, Mo.), who was shepherding the administration's bill, asked Bob Dole for a nose count. If 51 votes were in sight, he wanted to bring the Conrail bill up for floor action promptly. But when the Senate began its debate, Senator Howard Metzenbaum (D, Ohio) filibustered, effectively staving off any action during the 1985 session.

When the Senate majority finally prevailed in early 1986, the Morgan Stanley coalition apparently had lost. But the vote had shaken out a number of senators who weren't entirely comfortable with some parts of the deal. The controversy made it likely that a replay in the House would find a majority opposed to the merger. Representative John Dingell, the chairman of the House Energy and Commerce Committee, was waiting for the case to come to him. He appeared sympathetic to the public offering but had not made up his mind. To get a reading on how his constituents stood on the issue, he conducted an informal poll among Michigan's most important employers and freight forwarders.

Railroad competition – a telling factor

It was no surprise that the Michigan railroads – Grand Trunk, Western, and a short-line railroad in Ann Arbor – were against the sale to Norfolk Southern. Competition with Conrail and Norfolk Southern was tough enough. If Norfolk Southern owned another 528 route miles, railroading in Michigan would become a virtual monopoly. The steel industry and the utilities were just as militantly against it. If Conrail were to be absorbed by the Norfolk Southern, the railroads would no longer have to compete for their business. The survey was very important in the outcome of the eventual vote, but it was not enough to sway Dingell. He wanted to hear from the grassroots, and he wanted to be sure the other members of the Energy and Commerce Committee were with him.

To ensure that the other members of the committee heard from *their* constituents, the coalition cranked up a letter-writing campaign aimed at every representative on the committee except Dingell.

Some 5,000 letters were sent to retirees from the old Penn Central Railroad, who had a direct economic interest in the outcome of the fight. Their pensions would have been at risk if the number of present Conrail employees was cut – a distinct likelihood, since the Southern had promised cuts in wage and employee costs. (Like Social Security benefits, railroad pensions are funded by the payments of present employees into a railroad retirement fund; unlike Social Security, when the contribution pool goes down, so does the payout). The return on this campaign was immediate, as thousands of Mailgrams expressing concern about the Norfolk Southern purchase hit Washington.

At the same time, the Energy and Commerce Committee's financial advisers, Lazard Frères, assured Dingell that a public offering was a viable alternative to a direct sale. And even within the administration, opinions began to change. Goldman, Sachs, financial advisers to the Department of Transportation, had originally told Secretary Dole that a public offering wouldn't lure enough subscribers to pull off the sale. But the longer the investigation went on, the more Goldman, Sachs tended to believe that a public offering might work.

Farm interests provide the clincher

By the summer of 1986, John Dingell had enough assurances that his vote against the sale might be sustained. The clincher came when almost 1,100 national and state-level farm organizations announced that they, too, supported public ownership of Conrail. Ed Andersen, Master of the National Grange, recalls the moment with glee: "This was where the Grange came in more than a hundred years ago, working against a railroad monopoly."

In October, when Congress was ready to leave for its fall recess, the House Energy and Commerce Committee voted to approve public sale of Conrail. Norfolk Southern withdrew its bid.

Ironically, Morgan Stanley, the sparkplug of the opposition to the sale, almost lost out on the offering, as Goldman, Sachs was named the lead investment bank for the public offering. Quick action on the Hill took care of that, however. The law calls for no less than four, and no more than six, banks to float the issue. Morgan Stanley is right in there today, underwriting the Conrail issue it had worked so hard and invested in so heavily to bring about.

11

Resurrecting a Lost Cause

If you do lose the first round, take heart. A loss in Washington does not mark the end of the fight – just the close of a round. The fights go on and on, and even the round that has gone against you is bound to have made an impression on your opponents. You'll find that some of your ideas have been picked up along the way, and that will make it easier the next time around. And there *will* be a next time around.

Stay with it! Every two years brings a new Congress, and every four years a new administration. Political control changes, economic and social philosophies change, opponents sometimes mellow; the Supreme Court may make a decision which favors your side, or you may have learned a little more about how to win in Washington. Patience, eternal optimism, and a firm belief in the need for the change you are proposing are qualities essential to eventual success.

Senator William Proxmire (D, Wis.), champion of a coalition of civil rights and church groups pushing for Senate ratification of an International Genocide Treaty, delivered a speech at the beginning of every day's Senate session in support of the treaty. Only after some 3,000 such speeches, delivered over 30 years, did the Senate vote overwhelmingly to support the treaty, in 1986.

Keeping Your Issue in Play

Always remember that the legislative process moves with the speed of a glacier, and that experienced players measure time in two-year congressional sessions. As we saw earlier, it took 15 years, four presidents and eight Congresses to get a national water-projects bill passed in 1985. The struggle over federal regulations requiring airbags in motor vehicles has consumed an equivalent amount of time, and another five years of wrangling is in sight. By comparison, the six years spent by farm interests to get contract protection written into the revised Export Administration Act seems like an overnight success.

Changing tactics

Washington is populated with hundreds of trade associations and citizens' groups willing to wait years simply for committee chairmanships to change, in the expectation that their legislative day will arrive under new management.

People who have been around the track once in Washington don't even wait 24 hours before starting the next round with a new approach. So open a new legal pad and sketch out a new balance sheet. Go back through your files and see whether there was a crossroad at which you turned left when you should have gone right. Possibly your program was bottled up in the wrong committee. The nation's retail druggists were faced with that problem, and they came up with an effective solution.

The country's pharmacists wanted Congress to make it a federal crime to steal controlled substances during drug-store robberies. The chairman of the Judiciary Committee was adamantly against this measure, not because he thought that robbing a drug-store was a minor offense, but because he didn't want to make local stick-ups into federal cases that would clutter US district courts.

Amending the US Code made sense, the druggists argued. Most drug stores are held up because they offer twin enticements – ready cash, and drugs that could either be used or sold. If the robbers are caught outside the store in possession of the drugs, they are automatically charged with a federal crime; if they are caught in the act of robbing the store, however, they just have to deal with the local police.

The chairman was not impressed, and the bill languished for four years in committee. The druggists hired a new legislative counsel – and got what they paid for. The new counsel redrafted the bill so that it went to the Energy and Commerce Committee, rather than Judiciary.

The Commerce Committee liked the idea and decided to hold hearings. When the proceedings came to the attention of the Judiciary Committee, its chairman suddenly remembered (1) that this was a judicial matter and (2) that the proposal had been in his committee's back files for the past two Congresses. A mark-up session was scheduled immediately, and Judiciary reported it out for passage.

Biding your time

Even if your tactics were correct, perhaps you were swimming upstream the first time around. Help might be on the way. New administrations bring new directions – a fact that allowed the Big Three cereal companies to get the Federal Trade Commission off their backs after a five-year struggle so expensive that it deserves its own line in the Gross National Product. Congress was a very interested observer from beginning to end.

During the Carter administration, the FTC developed a novel legal theory charging the large cereal manufacturers with sharing a monopoly of the market by bottling up the display space in the supermarkets. The government spent millions of dollars preparing to prosecute on this theory. Our client, Kellogg's, and the other companies were prepared to defend right down to the last sugar crisp, so ridiculous did they consider the charges. The people actively involved included dozens of FTC lawyers, investigators, and economists on one side, and dozens of lawyers from blue-ribbon law firms, lobbyists (the Hill was always kept informed of the progress by both sides), public relations firms, and teams of researchers on the other.

When the case finally came before a hearing examiner, the atmosphere was like that of the opening of a Broadway show. Several young lawyers were standing in the doorway, discussing strategy and projecting how long it would take to extricate their huge clients from the government's clutches. "I'm going to send my kid through Harvard Law School on this case," said one of the attorneys, barely 30 years old. That was in 1978 and we had just finished sending a son through MIT on the same case (although he was well on his way before we had shared monopoly to sprinkle over our morning cereal.)

Then in 1981 the administration changed, and the regulatory mood shifted rapidly. Ronald Reagan did not want the government fooling around with supermarket shelves, and there was a Republican majority in the Senate. The government lost interest, and the FTC finally was glad to forget about the whole thing.

Diving into Think Tanks

If you can't find any flaws in your tactics and it doesn't look as if the philosophy of government is going to change radically enough to accommodate your ideas, it might pay to look into what the think tanks are doing and whether your ideas are compatible with the projects they are working on. Think tanks, staffed by intellectuals who receive public and private contracts to analyze ideas and project goals for government and industry, have a profound influence on the mood of the country. In due course, a high percentage of the output of the major think tanks influences government policy.

The books they produce are reviewed in the major media, and their ideas are accorded serious treatment. Their researchers are invited to take part in TV debates, asked to testify before Congress, and their upper- and mid-level personnel move comfortably in and out of government. When in government, they write position papers that reflect their think tank days. So, when an issue comes up for legislative or regulatory action, a body of academic work usually is at hand to support the views.

Ben Wattenberg, a scholar in good standing at the American Enterprise Institute, recalls that the groundwork for airline deregulation was set into place in the early 1970s at AEI. By the mid-1970s, the theories were going through a full-court press of information – articles, books, seminars, and hearings, all of them publicized aggressively.

"It was no accident that within a few years, legislation on deregulation was on the way," he says. "It is not a hidden-ball trick that gets policy changed in Washington."

The think-tank business has mushroomed in the last 10 years. Once there was just one, the Brookings Institution, which delivered opinion from on high – apolitical, unbiased, and implicitly believed by all, except conservatives, who considered it left-wing, slanted, and a nail in the coffin of the Republic. During the Reagan years, because of the many policy analysts who found shelter there, Brookings was called the Democratic government-in-exile.

But Brookings is always heard and always consulted by policy-makers, and it continues to play an influential role in congressional policy formation. The concept of a Congressional Budget Office sprang at least partially from its theorists, and one of its own scholars, Alice Rivlin, became the office's first director.

Brookings can still regally dismiss ideas it considers unworthy. A few years ago, Democrats alarmed that the United States was falling behind in international trade began to consider the idea of a government program to give guidance and direction on industrial policy to US manufacturers. Just one article by Brookings senior fellow Charles Schulze took care of that questionable concept. Schulze, who had been chairman of President Carter's Council of Economic Advisers, said the idea was not viable for the United States – and he said it not only in his own signed article, but also in an interview for Leonard Silk's influential economics column in *The New York Times*. The idea hasn't been heard from since.

In the 1970s, conservatives challenged Brookings' intellectual supremacy by flocking to the American Enterprise Institute, which quickly became a home away from home for corporate America. AEI gave intellectual underpinnings not only to airline deregulation, but also to such subjects as the beneficial effects of unchecked population growth in Third World countries and the predicted eclipse of the federal government as the primary agency of social policy in the United States.

From these two prototypes, myriad other research institutes have evolved, all of them financed by private contributions and all of them interested in seeing their research affect the system. The Heritage Foundation staked out its claim somewhat to the right of AEI and emerged as the conservative conscience of the Reagan Administration. The Center for Strategic and International Studies delves into foreign policy. One of the newest, the Institute for International Economics, has taken hold of global monetary matters.

The advantage that think tanks have over universities is that their scholars are frequently fresh from a high-level government job, so they know what will fly and how to get it into the air. The revolving door works the other way, too. When the Heritage Foundation's

Stuart Butler said that the White House would soon present a paper on the privatization of welfare, he knew what he was talking about. The person in charge of writing the report at the White House was his coauthor on a book on the subject and the person assisting the White House expert was a woman who worked for Butler until she joined the administration.

Think tanks depend on recognition and success of their ideas to keep funds rolling in. If their ideas are no more than a half-step ahead of the prevailing mood of the country, their chances of winning are great. If they are too far ahead, their chances of success – and of financial support – diminish. Even thinkers are paid by results.

"We are in the business of making ideas ready for legislation," says Stuart Butler, one of the leading planners at the Heritage Foundation, the far-right think tank that has had such a strong impact on the Reagan administration.

"So is every so-called think tank," he adds. "The difference between the Heritage Foundation and other institutions like us is that we work on a shorter time frame. We want ideas that will translate into action within a year or 18 months. We never, or very rarely, come up with completely new concepts. We work with evolving needs. We pinpoint them, develop them, bring them to the attention of the administration and, once they are in the hopper, go on to the next item on the agenda."

A good example is the concept of enterprise zones. The idea came from Great Britain, where Sir Geoffrey Howe suggested revitalizing British cities, hard hit by an economic slump, by forgiving or lessening taxes on new businesses. In the United States, some conservatives, including the President, thought the idea could be applied to economically depressed areas – principally urban slums and rural communities. But the story of this idea has as much to do with marketing as with brainpower.

"The idea was in the air, but it didn't seem to take hold in Congress," says Stuart Butler. "It seemed such a politically advantageous idea, but it just didn't get through. So we went back to the drawing board and decided that it would be a good idea for states suffering from the decline in manufacturing and agriculture."

Once the strategy was set in place, Heritage's public relations team swung into action, doing as good a job as any for-profit public relations agency. And the steps they took don't sound all that different from those a grassroots lobbyist would take. Newspapers described the advantages of enterprise zones. Speakers appeared in cities around the country to talk to business groups and service clubs about it. Local anchorpersons sent out film crews to show how a new business was breathing life into an abandoned building downtown.

Over time, the idea was accepted at the state level. Governors and mayors snipped ribbons to open factories that had been moribund and rotting. In the 30-odd states where enterprise zones were created, governmental charts showed the effect of the zones on the unemployment ratio in the area. All this activity put more pressure on Congress to adopt the idea on a federal level, where income-tax breaks are a powerful tool. The concept probably lost a notch of credibility when the 1986 tax reform bill did away with most tax breaks, but the Heritage machine is still plugging away – and in the meantime, state enterprise zones have been put into place across the country.

Butler compares the work of his foundation to the work of engineers, who take the seminal ideas of physicists and mathematicians and make some workable product out of it. "Ideas are beautiful, but they are only effective if they can be translated into action," he says. "That's what we are for."

Ideas do manage to seep into the public consciousness over a period of time. In 1948, a young reporter in Erie, Pennsylvania, interviewed Norman Thomas, the perennial Socialist candidate for the presidency. It was during the last of his six runs, all of which had a predestined outcome. Thomas was an old hand who knew that the reporter was looking for a snotty lead to a story when he inquired how the candidate reckoned his chances of winning.

"Well," he said, "when I first ran for president in 1928 I advocated revolutionary changes in American life. My platform called for unemployment insurance, paid holidays, five-day work weeks, minimum wages, and child labor laws. This year Governor Dewey's Republican conservative platform is more revolutionary. You might say I've already won."

Hang in! And good luck.

Further Reading

Lobbying

Overview

Bayless, Betty. *Citizens in Action* (St Paul, Minn.: The League, 1981).

Beauchamp, Katherine. *Fixing the Government* (Ringwood, Australia and New York: Penguin Books, 1986).

Berry, Jeffrey M. *Lobbying for the People* (Princeton, NJ: Princeton University Press, 1977).

Buffington, Erica. *Citizens in Action* (St Paul, Minn.: The League, 1985).

Collison, Koder M. *The Lobby . . . Vestibule for Action* (Kansas City, Mo.: American Industrial Development Council, 1978).

Cook, Fred J. *Lobbying in American Politics* (New York: Franklin Watts, 1976).

Crawford, Kenneth Gale. *The Pressure Boys* (New York: Arno Press, 1974).

Deakin, James. *The Lobbyists* (Washington, DC: Public Affairs Press, 1966).

Dexter, Lewis Anthony. *How Organizations are Represented in Washington* (Lanham, Md.: University Press of America, 1987).

Eastman, Hope. *Lobbying* (Washington: American Enterprise Institute for Public Policy Research, 1977).

Hall, David Roots. *Cooperative Lobbying* (Tucson: University of Arizona Press, 1969).

Horsky, Charles Antone. *The Washington Lawyer* (Westport, Conn.: Greenwood Press, 1981).

Howe, Russell Warren. *The Power Peddlers* (Garden City, NY: Doubleday, 1977).

Jaffe, Eliezer David. *Pleaders and Protesters* (New York: American Jewish Committee, Institute of Human Relations, 1980).

Kahn, Melvin. *A Lobbying Triumph* (Wichita, Kan.: Gerontology Center, Wichita State University, 1981).

Lewin, Tamar. *The Power Persuaders* (Washington, DC: Common Cause, 1978).

Lofland, John. *Crowd Lobbying* (Davis, Calif.: Institute of Governmental Affairs, University of California, 1982).

Malvern, Paul. *Persuaders* (Toronto and New York: Methuen, 1985).

Milbrath, Lester W. *The Washington Lobbyists* (Westport, Conn.: Greenwood Press, 1976).

Miller, Charles. *Lobbying Government* (Oxford and New York: Basil Blackwell, 1987).

Norwick, Kenneth P. *Lobbying for Freedom* (New York: St Martin's Press, 1975).

Sagstetter, Karen. *Lobbying* (New York: Franklin Watts, 1978).

Smith, Dorothy. *In Our Own Interest* (Seattle: Madrona Publishers, 1979).

Stanhope, Marcia. *A Political Initiative* (New York: National League for Nursing, 1980).

The Washington Lobby (Washington, DC.: Congressional Quarterly, 1987).

Williams, Karen Hastie. *Lobbying* (Washington, DC: Federal Publications Inc, 1984).

Wolf, Alvin. *Lobbies and Lobbyists* (Boston: Allyn and Bacon, 1976).

Interest-Group Politics

Adams, Gordon. *The Politics of Defense Contracting* (New Brunswick, NJ: Transaction Books, 1982).

Adams, James Lewis. *The Growing Church Lobbying in Washington* (Grand Rapids, Mich.: Eerdmans, 1970).

Bailey, Stephen Kemp. *Education Interest Groups in the Nation's Capital* (Washington, DC: American Council on Education, 1975).

Balitzer, Alfred. *A Nation of Associations* (Washington, DC: American Society of Association Executives, American Medical Political Action Committees, 1981).

Bauer, Raymond Augustine. *American Business & Public Policy* (Chicago: Aldine Atherton, 1972).

Braam, G. P. A. *Influence of Business Firms on the Government* (The Hague, NY: Mouton Publishers, 1981).

Browne, William Paul. *Private Interests, Public Policy, and American Agriculture* (Lawrence, Kan.: University Press of Kansas, 1988).

Chittick, William O. *State Department, Press and Pressure Groups* (New York: Wiley-Interscience, 1970).

Chubb, John E. *Interest Groups and the Bureaucracy* (Stanford, Calif.: Stanford University Press, 1983).

Corporate Government Relations and Lobbying (Philadelphia: American Law Institute–American Bar Association Committee on Continuing Professional Education, 1984).

Everson, David H. *Public Opinion and Interest Groups in American Politics* (New York: Franklin Watts, 1982).

Feldstein, Paul J. *Health Associations and the Demand for Legislation* (Cambridge, Mass.: Ballinger, 1977).

Greenwald, Carol Schwartz. *Group Power* (New York: Praeger, 1977).

Guither, Harold D. *The Food Lobbyists* (Lexington, Mass.: Lexington Books, 1980).

Harmon, Robert B. *Interest Groups and Lobbying in American Politics* (Monticello, Ill.: Council of Planning Librarians, 1978).

Heldman, Dan C. *Unions and Lobbying* (Arlington, Va.: Foundation for the Advancement of the Public Trust, 1980).

Herring, Edward Pendleton. *Group Representation Before Congress* (New York: Russell & Russell, 1967).

Hertzke, Allen D. *Representing God in Washington* (Knoxville: University of Tennessee Press, 1988).

Holtzman, Abraham. *Interest Groups and Lobbying* (New York: Macmillan, 1966).

Hrebenar, Ronald J. *Interest Group Politics in America* (Englewood Cliffs, NJ: Prentice-Hall, 1982).

Hubbard, Richard L. *Lobbying by Public Charities* (Washington, DC: National Center for Voluntary Action, 1977).

Interest Groups (Washington, DC: Government Research Corporation, 1977).

Leddy, Edward F. *Magnum Force Lobby* (Lanham, Md.: University Press of America, 1987).

Levitan, Sar A. *Business Lobbies* (Baltimore, Md.: Johns Hopkins University Press, 1984).

Levy, Elizabeth. *The People Lobby – The SST Story* (New York: Delacorte Press, 1973).

Lipsen, Charles B. *Vested Interest* (Garden City, NY: Doubleday, 1977).

McFarland, Andrew S. *Public Interest Lobbies* (Washington, DC: American Enterprise Institute for Public Policy Research, 1976).

Melone, Albert P. *Lawyers, Public Policy and Interest Groups Politics* (Washington, DC: University Press of America, 1977).

Miller, Robert Wiley. *Corporate Ambassadors to Washington* (Washington,

DC: American University, Center for the Study of Private Enterprise, 1970).

Miller, Stephen. *Special Interest Groups in American Politics* (New Brunswick, NJ: Transaction Books, 1983).

Ogene, F. Chidozie. *Interest Groups and the Shaping of Foreign Policy* (New York: St Martin's Press, 1983).

Ornstein, Norman J. *Interest Groups, Lobbying and Policymaking* (Washington, DC: Congressional Quarterly Press, 1978).

Public Opinion and Public Policy (Itasca, Ill.: F. E. Peacock Publishers, 1981).

Salisbury, Robert Holt. *Interest Group Politics in America* (New York: Harper & Row, 1970).

Scott, Susan Jane. *Lobbying for Health Care* (Rockville, Md.: American Occupational Therapy Association, 1985).

Trice, Robert H. *Interest Groups and the Foreign Policy Process* (Beverly Hills, Calif.: Sage Publications, 1976).

The Legislative Process and Political Dynamics

American Enterprise Institute for Public Policy Research. *Proposals to Revise the Lobbying Law* (Washington, DC, 1980).

Bills, Sharyn Sweeney. *Taking Part in the Legislative Process* (Chicago: AHA, 1978).

Brody, Ralph. *The Legislative Process* (Cleveland, Ohio: Federation for Community Planning, 1978).

Brook, William A. *Equilibrium in Political Markets on Pork-Barrel Issues* (Austin, Tex.: Graduate School of Business, University of Texas at Austin: distributed by the Bureau of Business Research, University of Texas at Austin, 1977).

Congressional Quarterly, Inc. *Legislators and the Lobbyists* (Washington, DC, 1968).

Dexter, Lewis Anthony. *The Sociology and Politics of Congress* (Chicago: Rand McNally, 1969).

Farkas, Suzanne. *Urban Lobbying: Mayors in the Federal Arena* (New York: New York University Press, 1971).

Fitch, Nancy Elizabeth. *Corridor Government* (Monticello, Ill.: Vance Bibliographies, 1982).

Haider, Donald H. *When Governments Come to Washington: Governors, Mayors and Intergovernmental Lobbying* (New York: Free Press, 1974).

Hayes, Michael T. *Lobbyists and Legislators* (New Brunswick, NJ: Rutgers University Press, 1981).

Holtzman, Abraham. *Legislative Liaison: Executive Leadership in Congress* (Chicago: Rand McNally, 1970).

Krebs, Frederick J. *Corporate Lobbying, Federal and State Regulation* (Washington, DC: Bureau of National Affairs, 1981).

Murphy, Thomas P. *Pressures Upon Congress* (Woodbury, NY: Barron's Educational Series, 1973).

Nader, Ralph. *More Action for a Change* (New York: Dembner Books, 1987).

Pearson, Drew. *The Case Against Congress* (New York: Simon and Schuster, 1968).

Renfro, William L. *The Legislative Role of Corporations* (New York: Presidents Associations, Chief Executive Officers' Division of the American Management Associations, 1983).

Schlozman, Kay Lehman. *Organized Interests and American Democracy* (New York: Harper & Row, 1986).

Smith, Hedrick. *The Power Game* (New York: Random House, 1988).

Truman, David Bicknell. *The Governmental Process* (Westport, Conn.: Greenwood Press, 1981).

Waage, Donn L. *Working with Government* (Minneapolis, Minn.: Northwest Bancorporation, 1979).

Zeigler, L. Harmon. *Lobbying: Interaction and Influence in American State Legislatures* (Belmont, Calif.: Wadsworth, 1969).

Zeller, Belle. *Pressure Politics in New York* (New York: Russell & Russell, 1967).

Money and Lobbying

Campaign Contributions and Lobbying Laws (Falls Church, Va.: Federal State Reports, 1980).

Common Cause. *How Money Talks in Congress* (Washington, DC: Common Cause, 1978).

Drew, Elizabeth. *Politics and Money* (New York: Macmillan, 1983).

Jackson, Brooks. *Honest Graft: Big Money and the American Political Process* (New York: Alfred A. Knopf, 1988).

Smith, Judity G. *Political Brokers: Money, Organization, Power and People* (New York: Liveright, 1972).

Stern, Philip M. *The Best Congress Money Can Buy* (New York: Pantheon Books, 1988).

How-to Guides

Alderson, George. *How You Can Influence Congress* (New York: Dutton, 1979).

Caplan, Marc. *Ralph Nader Presents a Citizens' Guide to Lobbying* (New York: Dembner Books, distributed by Norton, 1983).

DeKieffer, Donald E. *How to Lobby Congress* (New York: Dodd, Mead, 1981).

Gottlieb, Alan M. *Gun Owner's Political Action Manual* (Ottawa, Ill: Green Hill Publishers, 1976).

Heddesheimer, Janet C. *Government Liaison Worker and Handbook* (Falls Church, Va.: American Personnel and Guidance Association, 1979).

Hellebust, Lynn. *Resource Guide to Influencing State Legislatures* (Topeka, Kan.: Government Research Service, 1984).

Liberty Lobby. *The How* (Washington, DC, 1969).

Lustberg, Arch. *Testifying with Impact* (Washington, DC: Association Division, US Chamber of Commerce, 1982).

Manual for State Legislative Programs (New York: AICPA, 1982).

Mater, Jean. *Public Hearings, Procedures and Strategies* (Englewood Cliffs, NJ: Prentice-Hall, 1984).

National Association of Bar Executives. *Manual of Legislative Techniques* (Chicago, 1975).

Remmes, Harold. *Lobbying for Your Cause* (Babylon, NY: Pilot Books, 1986).

The Sierra Club Political Handbook (San Francisco: Sierra Club, 1972).

Vogel, David. *Lobbying the Corporation* (New York: Basic Books, 1978).

Reference Guides

American Medical Association. *Federal Key Contact Program* (Washington, DC).

Close, Arthur C., and Jody Curtis, eds. *Washington Representatives, Who Does What for Whom in the Nation's Capital* (Columbia Books). *Major national associations, labor unions, and US companies, registered foreign agents, lobbyists, lawyers, law firms and special-interest groups, together with their clients and areas of legislative and regulatory concern.*

Cohn, Mary, ed. *Congressional Quarterly, Inc. Almanac* (Washington, DC: Congressional Quarterly Inc., annual summary of the *Congressional Quarterly Weekly Report*). *Major congressional actions, including congressional voting records, lobby registration directory, presidential messages, and the elections.*

Common Cause.

Congressional Quarterly Weekly Report.

Congressional Information Service. An index to and abstract of all congressional hearings, public laws, joint conference reports etc.

Kingsley, Roger P. *Congressional Action Contact Network Handbook* (Rockville, Md.: American Speech–Language–Hearing Association, 1987).

Kranz, Roger, ed. *The Capital Source, Fall 1987: The Who's Who, What, Where in Washington* (National Journal Inc., 1730 M St., NW, Washington DC, 20036). *Issued twice a year. Contents: Government; Corporate; Professional; Media.*

National Journal.

New York Times Index (issued quarterly).

1986 Survey of State Laws on Lobbying & PACS (New York: AIA Law Publications, 1986).

Public Affairs Information Service. A monthly/yearly index to articles published concerning public affairs.

Sharp, J. Michael. *The Directory of Congressional Voting Scores and Interest Group Ratings* (New York: Facts on File Publications, 1988).

Vance, Mary. *Lobbying, a Bibliography* (Monticello, Ill.: Vance Bibliographies, 1982).

Wall Street Journal Index.

Washington Post Index.

Washington Media

American Enterprise Institute for Public Policy Research. *A Liberal Media Elite?* (Washington, DC, 1985).

American Enterprise Institute for Public Policy Research. *Press, Politics and Popular Government* (Washington, DC, 1972).

Callahan, Daniel, et al. *Congress and the Media: The Ethical Connection* (Hastings-on-Hudson, NY: Institute of Society, Ethics and the Life Sciences, the Hastings Center, 1985).

Crouse, Timothy. *The Boys on the Bus* (New York: Random House, 1973).

Hess, Stephen. *The Government/Press Connection* (Washington, DC: The Brookings Institution, 1984).

Hess, Stephen. *The Washington Reporters* (Washington, DC: The Brookings Institution, 1981).

Hess, Stephen. *The Ultimate Insiders* (Washington, DC: The Brookings Institution, 1986).

Hyer, Svennik. *The Politics and Economics of the Press* (London and Beverly Hills, Calif.: Sage Publications, 1975).

Juergens, George. *News From the White House* (Chicago: University of Chicago Press, 1981).

Kronewetter, Michael. *Politics and the Press* (New York: Franklin Watts, 1987).

Lang, Gladys Engel. *The Battle for Public Opinion* (New York: Columbia University Press, 1983).

Lasky, Victor. *It Didn't Start With Watergate* (New York: Dial Press, 1977).

Leonard, Thomas C. *The Power of the Press* (New York: Oxford University Press, 1986).

Nord, David Paul. *Newspapers and New Politics* (Ann Arbor, Mich.: UMI Research Press, 1981).

The Presidency and the Press (Austin, Tex.: The Lyndon B. Johnson School of Public Affairs, University of Texas at Austin, 1976).

Rivers, William L. *The Opinionmakers* (Westport, Conn.: Greenwood Press, 1983).

Rubin, Richard L. *Press, Party, and Presidency* (New York: W. W. Norton, 1981).

Small, William J. *Political Power and the Press* (New York: W. W. Norton, 1972).

Tataryn, Lloyd. *The Pundits* (Toronto: Deneau, 1985).

Vance, Mary A. *Government and the Press* (Monticello, Ill.: Vance Bibliographies, 1981).

Washington Black Book: The Directory to the Washington Press Corps (Lanham, Md.: Madison Books, 1988).

Grassroots Lobbying

Flanagan, Joan. *The Grassroots Fundraising Book* (Chicago: Contemporary Books, 1982).

Gosnell, Harold Foote. *Grass Roots Politics* (New York: Russell & Russell 1970).

Gundelach, Peter. *Grass Roots Organizations* (Aarhus, Denmark: Institute of Political Science, University of Aarhus, 1978).

Institute for the Study of Labor and Economic Crisis. *Grassroots Politics in the 1980's: A Case Study* (San Francisco: Synthesis Publications, 1982).

Jacobson, Gary C. *The 95th Congress and Its Committees* (Washington, Conn.: Center for Information on America, 1977).

Jensen, Richard J. *Grass Roots Politics* (Westport, Conn.: Greenwood Press, 1983).

Metz, Joseph E. *The Politics of People-Power* (Woodbury, NY: Barron's Educational Series, Inc., 1972).

Robertson, James, and John Lewallen, eds. *The Grass Roots Primer* (San Francisco: Sierra Club Books, 1975).

Sim, John Cameron. *The Grass Roots Press: America's Community Newspapers* (Ames, Ia.: Iowa State University Press, 1969).

Torrence, Susan Walker. *Grass Roots Government: The County in American Politics* (Washington, DC: R. B. Luce, 1974).

Government Publications and Congressional Hearings

United States Congress: House. Published in Washington by the US Government Printing Office.

Committee on Ways and Means. Subcommittee on Oversight. *Report and Recommendations on Lobbying and Political Activities by Tax-Exempt Organizations*, 1987. LC call number: KF4948.A25 1987a.

Committee on Government Operations. Legislation and National Security Subcommittee. *The New Proposed Revisions to OMB* Circular A–122, 1984. LC call number: KF27.G6676 1983n.

Committee on Armed Services. Subcommittee on Investigations. *Allegations of Improper Lobbying by Department of Defense Personnel of the C-5B and B1B Aircraft and Sale to Saudi Arabia of the Airborne Warning and Control System* 1983. LC call numbers: UG1123.U52 1983; KF27.A753 1982c.

Committee on the Judiciary. Subcommitee on Administrative Law and Governmental Relations. *Public Disclosure of Lobbying Activity*, 1979. LC call number: KF27.J832 1979.

Committee on Government Operations. Commerce, Consumer, and Monetary Affairs Subcommittee. *IRS Administration of Tax Laws Relating to Lobbying*, 1978. LC call number: KF27.G634 1978c.

Committee on the Judiciary. Subcommittee on Administrative Law and Governmental Relations. *Lobbying and Related Activities*, 1977. LC call number: KF27.J832 1977a.

Committee on the Judiciary. Subcommittee on Administrative Law and Governmental Relations. *Public Disclosure of Lobbying Act*, 1975. LC call number: KF27.J832 1975c.

Committee on Standards of Official Conduct. *Lobbying – Efforts to Influence Governmental Actions*, 1976. LC call number: KF27.S7 1975.

Committee on Ways and Means. *Legislative Activity by Certain Types of Exempt Organizations*, 1972. LC call number: KF27.W3 1972d.

Committee on Standards of Official Conduct. *Legislative Activities Disclosure Act*, 1971. LC call number: KF32.S7 1971.

Committee on Standards of Official Conduct. *Lobbying*, 1971. LC call number: KF27.S7 1971.

Committee on Standards of Official Conduct. *Regulation of Lobbying*, 1970. LC call number: KF27.S7 1970a.

United States Congress: Senate. Published in Washington by the US Government Printing Office.

Committee on the Judiciary. *Integrity in Post Employment Act of 1986*, 1986. LC call number: KF26.J8 1986F.

Committee on Governmental Affairs. Subcommittee on Intergovernmental Relations. *Uniform Lobbying Cost Principles Act of 1984*, 1984. LC call number: KF26.G6738 1984a.

Committee on Governmental Affairs. *Oversight on the 1946 Federal Regulation of Lobbying Act*, 1984. LC call number: KF26.G67 1983o.

Committee on the Judiciary. Subcommittee on Separation of Powers. *The Federal Neutrality Act*, 1984. LC call number: KF26.J874 1984.

Committee on Governmental Affairs. *Lobby Disclosure Act of 1979*, 1980. LC call number: KF26.G67 1979ao.

Committee on Governmental Affairs. *Lobby Disclosures Act of 1979*, 1980. LC call number: KF26.G67 1979ao.

Committee on Governmental Affairs. Subcommittee on Federal Spending Practices and Open Government. *Prohibiting Federal Funds to Lobby State and Local Legislatures*, 1979. LC call number: KF26.G6732 1979b.

Committee on Governmental Affairs. *Lobby Reform Act of 1977*, 1978. LC call number: KF26.G67 1977r.

Committee on Government Operations. *Lobby Reform Legislation*, 1976. LC call number: KF26.G8 1975j.

Committee on the Judiciary. Subcommittee on Administrative Practice and Procedure. *Open Communications Act of 1975, S. 1289*. 1976. LC call number: KF26.J833 1976c.

Publications by the Governmental Printing Office

Lobbying and Political Activities of Tax-Exempt Organizations 1987. LC call number: KF4948.A25 1987.

Congress and Pressure Groups, 1986. LC call number: JK1118.C59 1986.

United States General Accounting Office. *No Strong Indication the Restrictions on Executive Branch Lobbying Should Be Expanded* 1984. LC call number: KF4948.A846 1984.

Summary of Testimony on Legislative Activities ("lobbying"), 1972. LC call number: KF4948.A25 1972.

United States: President (1963–9: Johnson). *Public Participation in the Processes of Government*, 1967. LC call number: JK1991.A46.

A Summary of Lobbying Disclosure Laws and Regulations in the Fifty States (Washington, DC: Plus Publications, 1978). LC call number: KF4948.Z95 S94.

Index